Contents

CW01476882

Editor: Geoff Laws 0191 201 6281

Additional Research: The Journal reviewers

Design: Geoff Laws

Photography: The Journal photographers, Northumbria Tourist Board and contributors

Editorial assistant: Emma Penights

Published by Newcastle Chronicle and Journal Ltd, Groat Market, Newcastle upon Tyne NE1 1ED.

How to use this guide

All the information in this Guide was carefully checked between January and April 2002. However, we all know businesses come and go and the fortunes of restaurants vary. Some change owner or management and chefs move on: menus and opening times can alter, so although we have tried to make all the information as accurate as possible, it's advisable to phone before trying somewhere new.

The Guide is fully independent and advertisers have had no influence over the choice of entries or the descriptions.
Restaurants are included because the Editor and The Journal reviewers have visited them, rated and recommended them. Eating out is a subjective business and tastes vary. However, good quality is always recognisable whether it's in the service, the food or the surroundings.

The cost of meals varies widely: We have given each entry a price based on the average cost of a three-course meal, including half a bottle of house wine. Special menus, pizza-pasta dishes, happy hours and business lunches can make a big difference to the price and are usually a bargain. When eating at Oriental and Indian restaurants the banquet or set meal menus are often very good value and offer a good range of dishes .

The Guide has four sections, Northumberland, Tyne & Wear, Durham and Tees Valley. In each of these sections are entries for restaurants listed alphabetically by town, there are also tea room listings and maps. Each map is divided by a grid and every entry in the Guide has a map reference.

The Guide contains a number of report forms and we would appreciate it if you would take the time to fill one in. Although our reviewers travel around the area finding new places to eat and revisiting established businesses, there are still some we may have missed. If a favourite of yours has been omitted from the Guide, please fill in a report form and send it to us. A photocopy will be fine if you don't want to spoil the book. We will then check out your suggestion for future editions.

Key to Symbols:

Children welcome

Accessible/or partially accessible for wheelchair users

4

W hen you visit Northumbria you are spoilt for choice, not just by the tranquil countryside and beautiful and historic buildings, but also by the vast number of restaurants and cafés now on offer.

Whether you visit Tyne & Wear, County Durham, Northumberland or Tees Valley you will find hundreds of great places to eat from stylish cosmopolitan brasseries and bustling Italian cafés in the cities to traditional English tea rooms in the countryside.

This excellent choice of restaurants contributed towards Northumbria being awarded 'Best Short Break Destination' at the English Tourism Council Awards in 2002 for its accommodation, food and drink, entertainment and other world-class facilities.

To highlight what the region has to offer, this year's Journal Eating Out Guide is being sponsored by the Northumbria Tourist Board along with the Countryside Agency and One NorthEast with the aim of promoting the tourism industry across the region as well as the local economy in countryside areas.

Written and produced by a team of food critics at The Journal newspaper, the reviews give a credible and impartial insight into a cross section of restaurants to suit every budget and occasion.

As well as discovering our historic cities, visitors can also explore the beautiful and dramatic landscapes with numerous villages barely changed for centuries.

Blanchland, Northumberland

The Guide contains reviews ranging from the best restaurants to tea rooms offering home-cooked fresh produce all round the region.

We hope this Guide will become an essential companion to your eating out excursions in Northumbria and trust you will enjoy sampling the food...

For more information call the Great North Number on 0191 375 3043 or www.visitnorthumbria.com

Newcastle Gateshead culture 2008

NORTHUMBRIA TOURIST BOARD

he restaurant industry has changed dramatically since I set up my first restaurant in the Eighties. Eating out was something of an occasion and there was little choice for the consumer. The more casual and relaxed style of restaurant that you see more and more today just did not exist.

Today, thankfully, eating out is part of many people's daily lives and it has become an extremely popular leisure pursuit at whatever age. There's now plenty of choice to suit everyone's budget and palate and this is what I call progress.

People's tastes are changing and customers are becoming more interested in food, thanks partly to the media and what's now available in supermarkets. This also raises customer expectations and encourages restaurants to be imaginative in their offerings.

In addition, more and more restaurants are using fresh, local, seasonal ingredients in their cooking and I hope to see more of this in the future.

The North-East has an abundance of produce on its doorstep - there's plenty of prized fish such as turbot, halibut and monkfish which is available at a reasonable price, there's excellent game and some great farmhouse cheeses, just to name a few.

Terry Laybourne

I would like to see a series of producer networks developed in the future consisting of serious small-scale local food producers working closely with restaurateurs and chefs to utilise what we have in the region. Initiatives such as the one being set up by the Northumbrian Larder is just one example of the type of collaborations that could be formed.

Although the North-East sometimes suffers with its image, I think many visitors are often pleasantly surprised. We have lots to offer and an increasing amount of restaurants are serving creative, innovative dishes at extremely reasonable prices - something to be proud of.

Terry Laybourne owns Café 21 and Bistro 21 restaurants in Newcastle, Ponteland and Durham. He is also a consultant chef for Newcastle United Football Club.

Do You Care About Your *Local Heritage?*

Want to do something about it?

With lottery support the Countryside Agency is running a scheme to help you care and is looking for good local heritage projects community groups want to run. We can provide grants of between £3,000 and £25,000, and advice to help you get going.

Call: **0870 9000 401** *or visit our website at:* **www.lhi.org.uk**

Heritage Lottery Fund

Nationwide

The Countryside Agency

Good chefs are usually highly individual but one thing that can't be disputed is that the best meals are those prepared with the freshest ingredients. That goes for meat or fish, fruit or vegetables and that is just as true for the finest cuisine in a top restaurant as for a quick snack scrambled together in a suburban kitchen.

As people look for the freshest produce they are also taking an increasingly keen interest in where their food is coming from, how it has been grown, raised and reared, and how far it has travelled before reaching their table.

This guide is packed with information to help you find the perfect place to eat, and as well as leading city centre restaurants, bistros and cafes it also features farm shops, farm tea rooms and farmers markets.

Through its Eat the View initiative, the Countryside Agency is working to encourage people to think local and buy local. So when you next go out for a meal make a point of looking to see whether the menu features any regional specialities and local produce. That might mean discovering farm-made cheeses, locally-reared beef, lamb and pork or handmade ice cream.

And when you are out in the countryside visit farm tea rooms - much of the produce they serve is local, and often from their own farm.

If you enjoy what you eat - buy local produce from a farm shop or farmers market and cook it yourself. Farmers markets are springing up across the region and there is a full list on page 129.

Farmers market

Local North-East produce is distinctive for its quality, freshness and flavour. By buying local food, you are supporting the rural economy, and you are helping the environment by cutting out many thousands of miles of wasted journeys as food is transported up and down the country.

So when you go out for a meal, think about where your food has come from. If you can "eat local" you will taste the difference.

The Countryside Agency

9

Places to eat in Northumberland

Matfen Hall
COUNTRY HOUSE HOTEL

AWARD WINNING CONTEMPORARY FINE DINING

Situated close to Newcastle, the Library Restaurant at Matfen Hall is the perfect country setting for fine dining. Recently awarded two 'AA Rosettes' for the highest standard of cuisine and service, the Library is also an excellent venue for private celebrations and corporate parties. The fabulous A Là Carte and Table d'Hôte menus are available every evening or enjoy a traditional Sunday Lunch in wonderful surroundings.

Exquisitely furnished with book lined walls, the Library is much more than a hotel restaurant, take an aperitif in the Drawing Room before enjoying a genuine fine dining experience. For larger parties, Matfen's Great Hall is a magnificent venue with it's own private entrance ensuring exclusivity. For further information, a brochure, or to make a reservation, please contact:

Matfen Hall
COUNTRY HOUSE HOTEL

MATFEN HALL MATFEN NEWCASTLE UPON TYNE
TEL 01661 886500 FAX 01661 886055
Email info@matfenhall.com   Website www.matfenhall.com

12

A   B   C

Berwick-upon-Tweed

1

Ancroft

Holy Island

Cornhill-on-Tweed

A1

Bamburgh

Belford

Wooler

Beadnell

Doxford

2

A697

Craster

Cheviot Hills

Alnwick

Newton-on-the-Moor

Warkworth

Harbottle

A68

Weldon Bridge

A1

3

N O R T H U M B E R L A N D

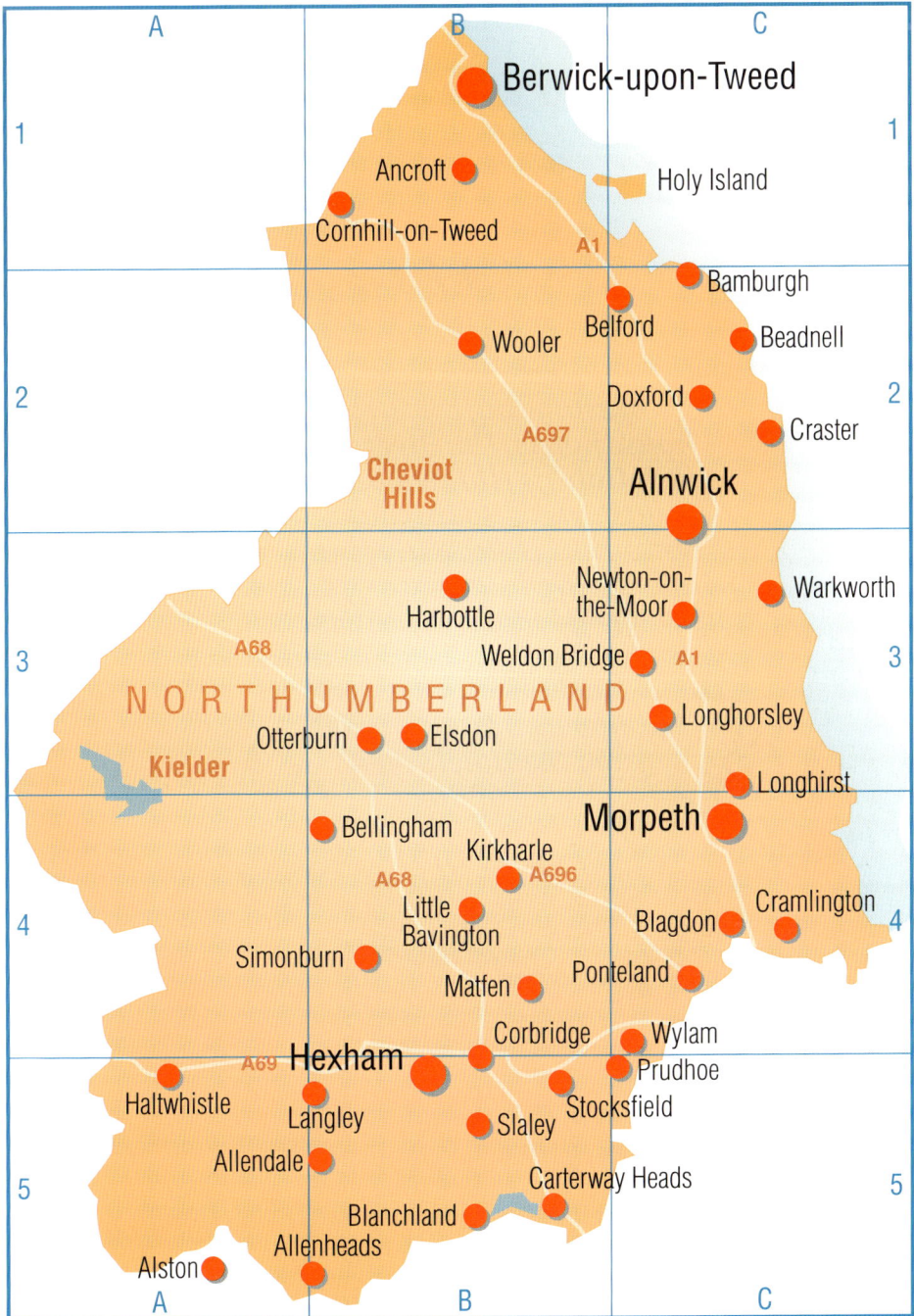

Longhorsley

Otterburn   Elsdon

Kielder

Longhirst

Bellingham

Morpeth

Kirkharle

A68   A696

Little Bavington

Cramlington

Simonburn

Blagdon

4

Matfen

Ponteland

Corbridge

Wylam

A69   **Hexham**

Prudhoe

Haltwhistle

Langley

Stocksfield

Slaley

Allendale

Carterway Heads

5

Blanchland

Allenheads

Alston

A   B   C

Riverdale Hall Hotel

Les Routiers
Gold Plate Award 2001

One of Northumbria's outstanding country house hotels, The Riverdale Hall Hotel is situated on the outskirts of Bellingham. The restaurant is elegantly furnished and offers a high standard of cuisine including regional specialities such as Kielder Venison, Northumbria Lamb, local Pheasant as well as Salmon and Trout caught from the Hotel's own stretch of River.

Riverdale Hall Hotel, Bellingham, Hexham, Northumberland
Tel: 01434 220254

Al Ponte

18, Front Street, **Corbridge**
01434 634214

Price £23

From the minute you step into this cosy, stone cottage you can feel the easy atmosphere. Relax into the comfortable leather chesterfields for your aperitif and browse through the menu and blackboard specials. There is a huge choice of pizza-pasta dishes which include a generous number of vegetarian options. The specials are where the chef establishes his personality with starters like Zuppa di pastinacca (roast parsnip and mild curry soup) and entrées like Pesce spada con limone e gamberetti (grilled swordfish steak in a lemon dill butter with capers and prawns). Desserts follow like summer after spring with Torta mandarino (oval mandarin slice with an orange and passion fruit couli). The Tuscan colours, candlelit tables and soft ambience make for a memorable and enjoyable experience.

Open: 7 days 12.00pm-2.00pm;
Mon-Sat 5.30pm-10.00pm;
Sun 6.00pm-10.00pm

Map ref: B5

The Angel Of Corbridge

Main Street, **Corbridge**
01434 632119

Price £26

The picturesque village of Corbridge has many attractions and The Angel is one of them. Blending ancient and modern this stylish restaurant is set in an historic coaching inn. The honey oak panelled reception area leads into the cool, clean contemporary lines of the dining room. The head chef has a pedigree including the Savoy and the Dorchester hotels in London, where he learned his art which he perfected and refined with Terry Laybourne of Café 21 fame. So, when you eat here you are eating haute chic. Start with Rare seared tuna salad with a Thai chilli dressing and move on to Breast of pheasant stuffed with apple and apricot, fondant potatoes and braised red cabbage. Finish the meal with Pineapple tart tatin with coconut ice cream. Early bird menus (2 courses £13.95 3 courses £16.00) offer a sample range of dishes.

Open:Mon-Sat 12.00pm-2.30pm;
Sun 12.00pm-3.30pm; Mon-Sat
6.00pm-9.30pm

Map ref: B5

Angler's Arms

Weldon Bridge, **Longframlington**
01665 570655

Price £22

Set in the heart of Northumberland, the Angler's Arms is an 18th century coaching inn with a 20th century Pullman railway carriage for a dining room. You can choose from the bar menu, which is highly regarded and very popular, especially at weekends with fishermen and walkers. If it's a little more style you want, try the a la carte menu in the 'Orient Express'. This offers a traditional selection of starters and main courses, local dishes made from local ingredients. All in all, the menu offers no surprises with straightforward, wholesome food at a good price.

Map ref: C3   Open: Mon-Sat 12.00pm- 2.00 pm & 6.30pm- 9.00 pm; Sun 12.00pm- 2.00 pm & 7.00 pm- 9.00 pm

Aphrodite Greek Restaurant

4, Brockwell Centre, **Cramlington**
01670 736070

Price £20

If you've had a Greek holiday the decor will bring it all flooding back. Fishing boats on the azure sea, old women in black and narrow cobbled streets of white-washed buildings create an unmistakable Hellenic atmosphere, helped along by the cheerful background bouzouki music and relaxed, friendly staff. On Friday evenings this is a lively, party restaurant where the dancing sometimes spills out onto the street. The Meze menu (Sun,Wed & Thurs) is great value with 18 dishes for £9.95 and the Happy Hour menu (Tues-Fri) offers a three course meal for £7.50. Live music and a broad range of interesting dishes make this worth a visit. A children's menu is available if your little ones are not into feta.

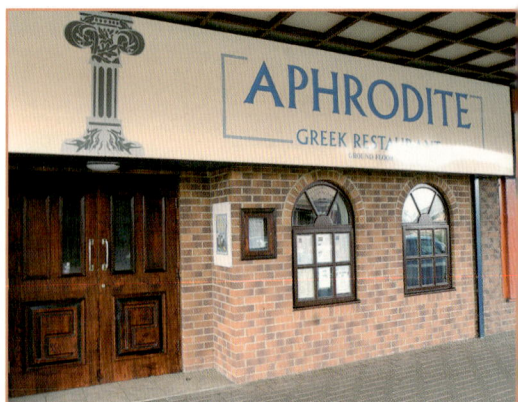

Map ref: C4   Open: Tues-Fri 5.30pm - 10.00pm Sat 6.00pm-10.00pm Sun 12.00pm - 2.00pm & 6.00pm -10.00pm

Benvenuti

1, Dorothy Forster Court, Narrowgate, **Alnwick**
01665 604465

Price £24

Situated in a splendid 18th century house in the shadow of Alnwick Castle's walls: the decor is rustic and the cuisine traditional. Small and cosy, family orientated with nine tables downstairs and another nine upstairs. The chefs create a range of pizza-pasta dishes plus the chicken, steak and fish standards. Specials change daily: the fish come in from Alnwick market or Amble each day. Lobster and Sea bass are popular as is the Pollo al Limone, chicken breast, white wine, butter, lemon juice and fesh herbs. Desserts are home-made. The menu carries a Kids' Corner for those who still resist anything foreign.

Open: Mon-Sat 12.00pm-2.00pm & 5.30pm-10.00pm.

Map ref: C2

The Blue Bell Hotel

Belford
01608 213543

Price £31

Belford village is an excellent base for a touring holiday of Northumberland. Close to the golden beaches of Northumberland and set in the heart of the rolling countryside it doesn't get much better than this. The Blue Bell Hotel, with its award-winning restaurant and very impressive wine cellar, is an extra bonus. The menus are adventurous, offering dishes from around the world. Starters such as Yoghurt and coriander sorbet with citrus fruits and mango sit comfortably alongside Seared tuna on roast vegetables with sun dried tomatoes and feta cheese. Entrées are equally imaginative with Breast of guinea fowl with bacon and whiskey cream and a sauté of pistachios and a broad range of seafood and meat dishes. The desserts are wonderful with Chocolate ganache rum torte and Honey tuiles of banana and nougat ice to tempt you off the straight and narrow. You could always walk it off tomorrow.

Open: 7 days 7.00pm-8.45pm last orders

Map ref: C2

Branches

Branch House, **Stocksfield**
01661 844264

Price £2€

Everything about Branches is tasteful and thoughtful. From the idyllic, country cottage exterior with blossom trees and roses in the garden to the bistro-chic menu, everything speaks of the care and personal touch of owner-sometime chef, Keith Mansell-Jarvis and his team. Three dining rooms wind their way through from the reception, each with a blackboard menu offering starters such as Apple and parsnip soup or the more extravagant King Orkney scallops pan-fried with a citrus butter sauce. Follow that with Rack of Northumberland lamb with rosemary and redcurrant sauce or Leek and gruyere tartlet with a fricassé of leeks and tomato and basil coulis. Home-made breads and real chips are available too. Finish off with the house speciality perhaps, Deep fried ice cream with a butterscotch sauce. You can have one, two or all three courses, but one visit will not be enough.

Map ref: B5   *Open: Tues-Sat 6.00pm-9.30pm,*
Sun 12.15-1.30pm

Café 21

35, The Broadway, **Ponteland**
01661 820357

Price £29

An informal restaurant with the emphasis upon relaxed dining, Cafe 21 offers top quality food at reasonable prices. Being one of Terry Laybourne's group of restaurants, it benefits from his guiding hand and the excellent standards that characterise his sister outlets. The bent beechwood chairs and closely set tables create a busy, cafe-style atmosphere. While the blackboard menus are part of the cafe experience, they do present a challenge for those with less than 20/20 vision. A minor quibble and not one to detract from the overall plaudits that Cafe 21 richly deserves. The menu offers a wonderful range of dishes: it's almost to difficult to choose just one for each course.

Map ref: C4   *Open: Mon-Fri 5.30pm-10.30pm;*
Sat 12.00pm-2.00pm
& 6.00pm-10.30pm

Canty's Brig Inn

Paxton, **Berwick-upon-Tweed**
01289 386255

Price £20

The restaurant stands on the banks of the river White Adder, in a beautiful part of Northumberland. Open fires in winter and terrace meals in summer make this a restaurant for all seasons. The menu has a range of traditional, British recipes plus a good selection of cosmopolitan dishes, all made from local ingredients. This combination of classical and continental means you are spoilt for choice. Kromerski (chicken, mushroom and garlic wrapped in bacon and deep fried in beer batter), Loin fillet of Border lamb with raspberry and red wine jus, Fresh Eyemouth scampi - all in generous servings for hearty country appetites. It takes a very hungry person to manage three courses but some do go on and attempt one of the delicious desserts on offer. The relaxed bistro style of this delightful restaurant provides an additional pleasure to a walk in the countryside.

Open: Summer 7 days 11.30am-2.30pm & 5.30-late: Winter closed Sun-Tues.

Map ref: B1

Cook and Barker Inn

Newton on the Moor
01665 575234

Price £25

A traditional stone-built country inn with elevated views over a Northumbrian coast. This well established pub serves good English cuisine and has raised the standard of its food to restaurant level. Lunch and evening menus carry a broad range of dishes, something to appeal to every palate. Starters like Lightly crumbed Brie fried and set onto garlic and herb butter, mushrooms with cranberry and port wine jelly, show a dash of imagination. Main courses offer fish, grilled and roast meats, oriental dishes and a 'Forest and Fields' selection which includes venison and chicken with lobster. Desserts change regularly. The fact that it's constantly winning Good Food awards means you may need to book as much as four weeks in advance - and a year ahead if it's Christmas lunch you want.

Open: 7 days 12.00pm-2.00pm & 7.00pm-9.00pm

Map ref: C3

Award winning cuisine
at LINDEN HALL

In the heart of beautiful Northumberland

The Dobson Restaurant at Linden Hall, has been awarded two 'AA Rosettes' for the highest standard of creative cuisine.

Serving the highest standard of regional, English and international cuisine, using only the finest and freshest ingredients, The Dobson Restaurant boasts two 'AA Rosettes' and breathtaking views across the Northumbrian coastline.

Linden Hall's own pub, The Linden Tree, is situated within the beautiful grounds of the estate and has all the charm and atmosphere that you'd expect from a traditional country inn. Perfect for a drink, lunch or dinner in relaxed and informal surroundings.

To make a reservation or for further details, please contact:

LINDEN HALL

Linden Hall Longhorsley Morpeth Northumberland
Tel 01670 50 00 00 Fax 01670 50 00 01
E-mail stay@lindenhall.co.uk   Take a virtual tour of Linden Hall at www.lindenhall.co.uk

Corbridge Tandoori

8, Market Place, **Corbridge**
01434 633676

Price £21

Looking down on the ancient market square of Corbridge, this restaurant with its beamed ceiling and local watercolours is vaguely reminiscent of an English tearoom - which it was in a former life. The cream and pink decor provides a comfortable setting for this easy-going, popular restaurant. It offers a wide range of dishes from all the regions of the sub-continent. Everything from Chicken tikka through Tandoori king prawns to Vegetable biryani. There are ten speciality curries including Murgh Makhani, a rich chicken dish cooked with almond nut powder, butter and cream and more than a dozen dishes recommended by the chef. With a host of side dishes and sundries, whatever they do, they do very well.

Open: 7 days 6.00pm-11.30pm   Map ref: B5

Danielle's Bistro

12, Eastgate, **Hexham**
01434 601122

Price £22

Set just off Hexham's main street, Danielle's Bistro is a pocket Italy in the heart of Northumberland. With its stripped wooden floors, country-style tables and chairs and exposed brick walls you can feel the warmth of the restaurant's rustic theme. Two big old fireplaces, crammed with ceramic pots and beamed ceilings add to the charm. No pizza-pasta is the first strong statement here. Everything comes off the blackboard, which has about fourteen choices for each course and be prepared for frequent changes. Starter: Coarse rustic duck, beef, pork terrine pate and apricot chutney. Main courses: Marinated venison casseroled in port and herbs and puff pastry. Desserts are part of the package and have a continental profile. The cellar offers a good range of wines.

Open: Mon-Sat 10.00am-2.00pm   Map ref: B5
& 6.00pm-10.30pm last orders

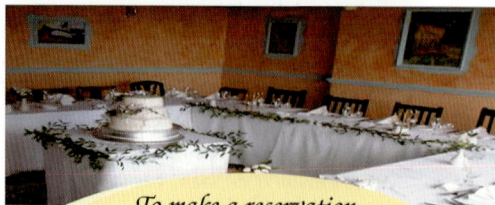

De Vere Slaley Hall - The Restaurant

Hexham
01434 673350

Price £39

Set in one thousand acres of prime Northumberland forest surrounded by two championship golf courses, Slaley Hall is a grand retreat. The elegant building houses one of Northumberland's finest restaurants with all the luxury you would expect of a hotel of this stature. The dining room has beautiful views over the fairways. The decor of muted yellows and gold with frosted glass panels provide pockets of intimacy in this spacious restaurant. The haute cuisine menu offers dishes such as Chicken, wild mushroom and truffle sausage, red wine and thyme sauce. For a main course Roast halibut fillet, foie gras, buttered linguine or one of a range of roasts and grills. Desserts are equally sophisticated: Iced blackberry parfait, apple fritters and Calvados sabayon or Northumbrian farmhouse cheeses. A lovely setting for a special treat.

Open: 7 days 7.00pm-9.15pm; Sun 1.00pm-2.00pm

Map ref: B5

Gi-Gi's

7, Newmarket, **Morpeth**
01670 512201

Price £25

Giovanni and Giuliano's (Gi-Gi's) restaurant is so much more than a pizzeria. The small street door belies the grandeur of the tented dining room. Booking does not guarantee you a table at the designated time, so be prepared to wait. The chefs' reputation for generous servings of beautifully cooked traditional dishes make this a very popular restaurant in Morpeth. The menu carries a good range of vegetarian, poultry, fish and meat dishes alongside the usual pizza-pastas. Although you will almost inevitably have to wait for your table, the regulars recommend you do because, at the end of it, the meal makes it all worth while.

Open: Thurs -Sat 12.00pm-2.00pm Mon-Sat 5.30pm-

Map ref: C4

Gianni's

3, Market Place, **Morpeth**
01670 511547

Price £23

Unmistakably Italian; Chianti bottles harbour red candles, ersatz vines cluster round the bar and teracotta walls combine to create a rustic, Tuscan feel. Bookings are not accepted and queuing on the stairs is the order of the day (evening) at weekends, which may test your dedication. The music is loud, the atmosphere and organisation chaotically friendly and the food, when you get it, is very good. House specials from the blackboard, such as Fresh mussels steamed with white wine and butter and Baked chicked breasts with green olives and Mozzarella and pesto sit alongside a full regular menu. It is a busy, bustling restaurant with a strong party feel.

Map ref: C4

Open: Mon-Sat 11.30am-2.00pm
& 5.30pm-11.00 pm,
Sunday 11.30am-2.00pm
& 7.00pm-10.00pm.

Henri's Brasserie

59, Bridge Street, **Morpeth**
01670 516205

Price £25

"Real food for real people" is the maxim of Henri's. The interior provides a modern background for the gloriously cosmopolitan menu. Dishes from every corner of the Earth feature, from Classic Caesar salad to Tempura of King prawns, Peppered black pudding to Pork kebabs, it's all there and rich desserts to boot. Starters such as Crostini of grilled goats cheese with leaf salad and Cumberland sauce are recommended, as is the ever popular Medallions of roast beef fillet on rosti with marsala sauce. There are plenty of vegetarian options, such as Risotto of asparagus and sweet peppers and various pasta dishes with tomato or cream based sauces. The wine list travels along with the menu and offers wines from around the world. Why go further when you can tour from your table?

Map ref: C4

Open: Wed-Sun 6.30pm-9.30pm,
Sat-Sun 10.30am-2.30pm

Il Piccolo

34, West Road, **Prudhoe**
01661 830389

Price £25

Just a hint of crazy but kept under control, chef/owner Emanuele has magpie tendencies - he collects everything. He was banned from going to the local bric-a-brac shop after the last time when he returned with a massive ship's lantern! His collection has to be seen to be believed. This very comfortable, relaxed restaurant is quietly confident and assured, and that goes for the food too. The number of dishes on the set menu competes with the specials and they are all very inviting. Fat and juicy King prawns in white wine and lemon sauce or Perra al Dolcelatte with the sweet crunchy fruit offset by the rich bite of the cheese. Entrées have the same interesting combinations, like Chicken breast stuffed with leek mousse and bacon in a cream sauce or Roasted monkfish with lemon in a white wine and dill sauce. Desserts galore and a very good humoured head waiter make for an entertaining and enjoyable night out.

Open: Mon - Sat from 7.00pm.   Map ref: C5

Kings Arms Hotel - Il Porto Di Mare

Hide Hill, **Berwick-upon-Tweed**
01289 307454

Price £22

The medieval, walled town of Berwick is skirted on one side by the river Tweed and miles of beach and sea on the other. The Kings Arms Hotel is a striking 18th century building with a 21st century restaurant. The dining room's decor combines cream with chrome, warm beechwood floors with black leather chairs and a stylish menu to match. No fish and chips here, but you can get Thai crab cakes with chilli and sour cream or Lemon sole with beurre blanc. There are plenty of poultry and meat dishes like Duo of game with caramelised plums and apricot jus. Vegetarian dishes are equally imaginative with pancakes or a mushroom strognanoff as main courses and starters like Warm goats cheese, herb crust, baby spinach and puy lentils. There's plenty of choice whatever your taste.

Open: Mon-Thurs 12.30pm-
2.00pm & 7.00pm-9.30; Fri-Sat
7.00pm-10.30pm last orders   Map ref: B1

Benvenuti
Italian
Restaurant

- Small cosy traditional Italian restaurant with rustic decor

- Wide range of pizza and pasta dishes and many "specials"

- Fresh fish (including sea bass and lobster) from Amble every day

- Home-made desserts

- Fully air-conditioned

We are open 6 days a week
12 noon to 2.00pm and 5.30pm - Last orders 10.00pm.
Happy hour 5.30pm - 6.30pm
Closed all day Sunday

Benvenuti
1 Dorothy Forster Court, Narrowgate, Alnwick
Telephone 01665 604465
Fax: 01665 605079

La Famiglia

20-22 St Mary's Chare, **Hexham**
01434 601700

*rice £22

Situated in a narrow, winding lane leading onto Hexham market place, La Famiglia occupies the upstairs rooms of what used to be monks' quarters. The entrance is easily missed so look out for a tricolour banner. Inside, creamy stone walls are embellished with a striking copy of a Michaelangelo. The owners are renowned for their friendliness giving the whole place a relaxed, party atmosphere. The menu carries the usual pizza-pasta dishes plus a range of fish, game and chargrilled dishes, some with a Mexican twist. A little out of the ordinary are dishes like Local Bangers and creamy mash and for a litle extra flair King prawn Filomena in garlic, white wine, lemon and vodka, flambéed at your table.

*Open: Mon-Sat 12.00pm-2.30pm
5.30pm-11.15pm*

Map ref: B5

Langley Castle

Langley-on-Tyne, **Hexham**
01434 688888

*rice £37

This crenellated, 14th century castle, deep in the valley forest of Tynedale, has all the romance and history anyone could ask for - and an award-winning restaurant to boot. Not surprising then that people are drawn there for special celebrations, weddings and so on, and for a dinner with a difference. The rather flowery language on the menu decribes starters like Aubergine fritters in a light herb batter served around a timbale of orange scented couscous and moated by a tomato and basil sauce. Setting the flummery aside, the Seared king scallops and black pudding with mashed potato, wilted spinach and white wine and lemon butter should please, as will the entrée Beef Cadwallader, a Northumbrian fillet griddled and carved with potato and shallot galette with king prawns and bordelaise sauce. Desserts are equally satisfying, there is a well-stocked vegetarian menu and everything is made to order.

*Open: 7 days 12.00pm-2.00pm;
.00pm-9.00pm last orders*

Map ref: B5

Linden Hall Hotel - Dobson Restaurant

Longhorsley
01670 516611

Price £3

A Georgian country house with extensive grounds in the heart of rural Northumberland. Elegant and luxurious, the dining room has panoramic views over the golf course towards the coast. The menu is very sophisticated and cosmopolitan. Confit of guinea fowl with bok choi, spring onions and ginger sit next to Grilled Toulouse sausage with a lentil and potato cake and red onion Lyonnaise. Desserts like Baked blueberry and lime tart surrounded by a stem ginger Anglaise sauce all at £24.50 make eating here a very affordable treat. No denims are allowed so wear your best bib and tucker.

Map ref: C3   *Open: 7 days 12.00 pm-2.00 pr*
                              & 7.00 pm-9.30 pr

Longhirst Hall - Boyson Restaurant

Longhirst
01670 795157

Price £2

The luxurious hotel, conference centre and golf course is set in acres of landscaped parkland. The dining room has a gallery and vaulted ceiling with a relaxed and convivial atmosphere. Various party night and corporate menus are available, plus other set menus. The a la carte offers an excellent range of dishes. A change of chef has seen Italian and Middle Eastern influences creeping into the menu like Apricot tart, Turkish delight ice cream and warm black cherries. There is now a fresh pasta section with, for example, Porccini mushroom filled ravioli topped with wild mushrooms; and vegetarians have their own menu with an invitation to vegans to have the chef tailor a dish specially for them. Why not stay overnight and enjoy the breakfast too?

Map ref: C3   *Open: Sun-Fri 12.00pm-2.00pr*
                              Mon-Sun 7.00pm-9.30pr

Lord Crewe Arms

Blanchland
01434 675251

rice £32

Beautiful Blanchland, the listed village, has many attractions, and the Lord Crewe is one of them. This 12th century monastery with its walled garden and ghost is the perfect base for a walking weekend with wonderful food. Diners are offered a four course dinner; Wood pigeon sautéed and served on stir fried vegetables with Madeira sauce and local Pork, tomato and basil sausages with parmesan mash and red onion compote set the standard. After soup or sorbet, move on to Medallions of venison with tangy redcurrant, orange mustard and port wine sauce or Carrot and cashew nut loaf with fresh herbs and gooseberry purée flavoured with rosemary. Desserts and rum truffles with your coffee and you'll need another walk. It's worth it though.

Open: 7 days 7.00pm-9.15 last orders;
Sunday 12.30pm-2.00 last orders

Map ref: B5

Manor House Inn

Carterway Heads, nr. **Shotley Bridge**
01207 255268

rice £23

The views across Weardale from this country inn are glorious. In winter the log fire gives a warm welcome but the friendly atmosphere is an all-year-round feature. Although a pub setting, the menu is anything but pub food - as you'll see. Mediterranean vegetables and goats cheese en croute or Parsnip and spiced apple soup make that clear. Entrées include steak, duck and salmon dishes. The Chicken in port wine with rosemary and herb sauce is recommended as is the Prawns in ginger with mange tout and smoked bacon salad. It just gets better and better. Desserts are rich and creamy with the ubiquitous Sticky toffee competing with Almond cake with a Baileys and white chocolate sauce. The chef uses local ingredients and cheeses and everything is home-made. You can taste the difference between this pub and the rest - which is why you should go.

Open: 7 days 12.00pm-2.30pm;
Mon-Sat 7.00pm-9.30pm last orders;
Sun 7.00pm-9.00pm last orders

Map ref: B5

Marshall Meadows Country House

Berwick-upon-Tweed
01289 331133

Price £2

England's most northerly hotel, set in the rolling Borders countryside, close to some of Northumberland's finest beaches - a lovely setting for a quiet weekend and very good food. The winding drive leads you through wooded grounds to this gracious Georgian mansion. The dining room is on two levels; the oak panelled room on the first floor has sweeping views down to the sea. The menu reflects the chef's interest in using local ingredients. Northumberland cheese and broccoli soup with herb croutons and Medallions of Borders beef with couscous, onion marmalade and rich red wine jus being two examples. Coconut cream on a passion fruit coulis stretch the desserts' horizons. Coffee in the very comfortable lounge and you can sit back and be lord of the manor - in your dreams.

Map ref: B1   *Open: 7 days 12.00pm-2.00pm*
6.30pm-9.00pm last order

Matfen Hall - The Library Restaurant

Matfen
01661 886500

Price £3

Matfen Hall is a splendid country house and golf club in acres of beautiful parkland. Aperitifs on a sumptuous sofa before a real log fire, dinner in the old library dining room, followed by coffee and petit fours back on the sofa- how the other half used to live! This award-winning restaurant justly deserves all the plaudits it receives. From the "Ladies-who-lunch" to the wedding breakfast, from local produce to exotic ingredients, everything is of excellent quality. Starters like Beef carpaccio with truffle oil and parmesan shavings or Salad of avocado and crab with pink grapefruit dressing demonstrate the range and imagination at work. Entrées such as Thyme roasted poussin with confit garlic and shallots lead on to desserts to die for. Plum creme brulée or Iced banana parfait with caramelised bananas ... maybe a round of golf before you start might be a good idea.

Map ref: B4   *Open: Mon- Sat 7.00pm-9.30 pr*
last orders; Sun 12.00pm-2.30pr

Milecastle Inn

Military Road, Haltwhistle
01434 320682

rice £22

A traditional, rural pub with stone walls, copper kettles and views for miles and miles over rolling Northumberland countryside. What more could you ask? Well, maybe a good meal? You'll certainly get good English food here, with a menu that would satisfy the heartiest walker. Sticky chicken fillets served with a honey glaze and salad garnish, or maybe the ubiquitous Thai fishcakes with a sweet chilli sauce dip to start. Follow that with Hunters Haunch, that's a 12oz sirloin steak stuffed with home-made paté, or perhaps the Duck breast stuffed with wild mushrooms in a rich plum sauce. If you still have room there is a selection of desserts and English and continental cheeses. In winter there is a roaring log fire so you can sip your coffee and bask in the glow.

pen: Wed-Sat 7.00pm-9.00pm;   Map ref: A5
un 12.00pm-2.00pm

New Beadnell Towers Hotel - The Tower Bistro

Beadnell
01665 721211

rice £28

The winding lanes of Beadnell village are highly picturesque and to find a restaurant of the stature of the Towers Bistro is a bonus. This ultra-modern restaurant with its vibrant colours and clean lines is a world away from the seaside café of my youth - and your's probably. After a brisk walk along the beach you can tuck into a plate of Seahouse smoked salmon with mixed leaves and a dill dressing followed by Char-grilled sirloin steak with horseradish butter, green salad and fries. There's plenty of choice but, moving on to desserts, why not have the Pear and almond tart with rich chocolate ice cream or Sticky toffee pudding with walnut and toffee sauce - or both? There is also an impressive array of local cheeses, like the famous Brinkburn goats cheese and the Northumbrian nettle, a tangy little number.

pen: Wed & Thur 7.00pm-9.30pm;   Map ref:C2
ri & Sat 7.00pm-10.00pm;
un 12.00pm-3.00pm

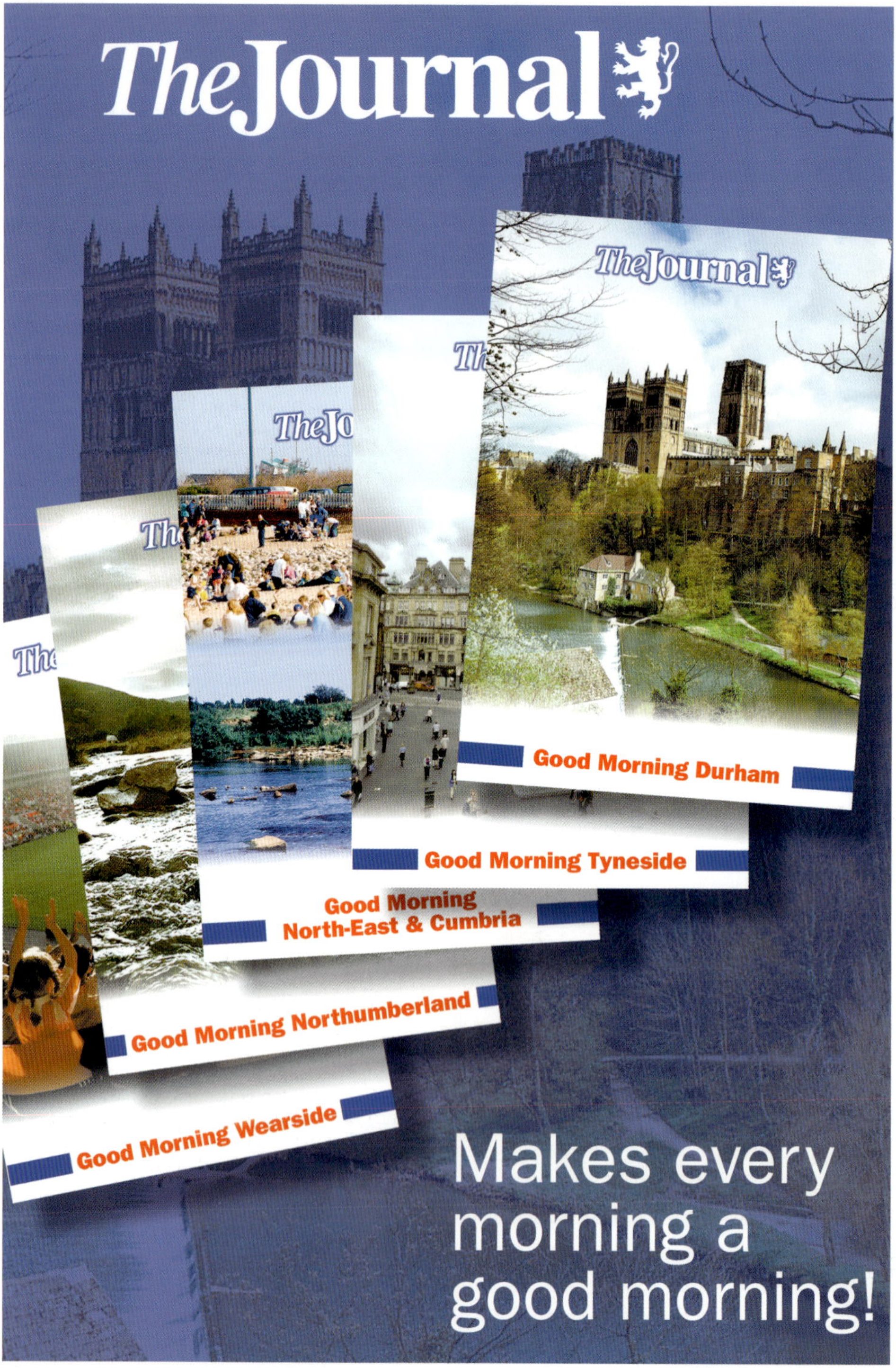

The Journal

Good Morning Durham

Good Morning Tyneside

Good Morning
North-East & Cumbria

Good Morning Northumberland

Good Morning Wearside

Makes every
morning a
good morning!

Otterburn Tower

Otterburn
01830 520620

ice £25

This distinctive, fortified country house, built by a cousin of William the Conqueror no less, stands in 32 acres of rolling parkland. The interior has all the charm and character that its history has bestowed with massive fireplaces with log fires, wonderful oak-panelled walls and mullioned windows. The dining room, in deep pink and golds, carries on the theme of comfort and confidence. The menu offers classic dishes with a twist, like Fricasse of pheasant with brandy cream sauce and Seared haggis with puree of swede and red wine jus to follow. There's more than a hint of luxury in the Pan-fried supreme of salmon, truffled risotto and chive cream sauce, but that is the hallmark of this restaurant. Desserts like Champagne and mandarin tart don't let the side down either. Local cheeses are a special feature. A lovely setting for a weekend walking break.

pen: 7 days 12.00pm-2.00pm &
.00pm-9.00pm

Map ref: B3

The Ramblers Country House Restaurant

Farnley, **Corbridge**
01434 632424

ice £30

Nineteenth century country house, just outside Corbridge, run by chef-proprieter Heinrick Hermann and his wife Jennifer. A la carte and set menus for every month of the year (two courses plus coffee £16.95, three courses plus coffee £19.95) include such delicious offerings as Goose liver paté with rum-soaked peaches and toasted brioche alongside Pan-fried medallions of monkfish and slow roast cherry tomatoes on dill sauce, all served by a head waiter who should win the waiter of the year award. Open log fires crackle on winter evenings - in summer the elegant dining room opens onto the gardens: you can even get married there. Why hold back?

pen: Tues- Sat from 7.00pm;
unday lunch from 12.30pm

Map ref:B5

David Ridle
Ridley's Fish and Game, Corbridg

come and
DISCOVER OUR HOSPITALITY

You're spoilt for choice when you visit Northumbria, not just by the tranquil countryside and historic cities, but by th wealth of restaurants on offer across the region.

As well as the hundreds of places to eat in Northumbria, why not take a trip out into the countryside and discover ou quaint village tea rooms and farm shops?

Overflowing with traditional fayre, they serve delicious home-cooked food using recipes that have been passed down through the centuries and reveal the true flavour of Northumbria.

For more information call the Great North Number on **0191 375 3043.**
www.visitnorthumbria.com

NORTHUMBRIA
TOURIST BOARD

Riverdale Hall Hotel Restaurant

Bellingham
01434 220254

Price £23

Open: 7 days 6.45pm-10.00pm

Map ref: A4

Riverdale Hall, a Victorian country house situated in the ruggedly picturesque countryside of the North Tyne valley, has the best of all worlds. Hill walking, salmon fishing, golf, horse-riding - all of which will guarantee a healthy appetite for the pleasures of the award-winning restaurant. The chef specialises in Thai cuisine but can equally skilfully turn his hand to more traditional dishes, as the menu shows. Local produce features strongly in dishes such as Smoked mackerel fishcakes griddled and served with crisp dressed salad and horseradish cream dressing. Entrées range from Roast rump of beef served with Yorkshire pudding and rich onion gravy to the more exotic Khaeng keeowan gai-green Thai chicken curry enriched with coconut milk. Desserts are home-made and the cheeses produced locally. No wonder this is a very popular venue for locals and holidaymakers alike.

The Smithy's Bistro

3, Bell Villa, **Ponteland**
01661 820020

Price £25

Open: Mon-Fri 12.00pm-2.30pm;
Mon-Thurs 6.00pm-10.00pm last
orders; Fri &Sat 6.00pm (Sat 5.30pm)
-11.00pm; Sun 12.00pm-4.00pm

Map ref: C4

A converted 19th century forge with original features: now a relaxed restaurant, popular with the Ponteland locals. The menu is a mix of traditional and modern with an interesting vegetarian selection. Waiters know their stuff, no distant blackboards, they memorise the specials: crisp and polished tableware with service to match. Starters like Fresh asparagus rolled with parma ham, served warm, drizzled with lemon beurre blanc and main courses such as Caramelised pork loin served with an apple scone and calvados sauce, are very tasty. The Magret duck breast with black cherry sauce with a hint of lavender honey is recommended. Seafood dishes vary according to the day's catch and there are plenty of grilled steaks, fish and lobster dishes. Desserts range from Northumberland cheeses and fruit through to a very decadent Chocolate fondue a la Suisse (for two).

The Tankerville Arms Hotel

Wooler
01668 281581

Price £2?

This fine old coaching inn in the heart of north Northumberland has two restaurants; the more formal Cheviot Restaurant and the Chillingham Bistro for a relaxed meal out. Having said that, both have a friendly, welcoming atmosphere and hotel guests and non-residents are often treated to a party night with themed evenings and menus to match. The cuisine is mainly traditional British dishes with a cosmopolitan flourish. Duck and port paté can be followed by Jamaican chicken (chicken cooked with ginger, pineapple and peppers in white rum and cream sauce) and finished off with New York Sundae (coffee ice cream with maple syrup and cream) made with locally produced ice cream. The Friday and Saturday night specials are very good value and show just how enthusiastic the team of owner, Anne Park, and her chefs are about their art.

Map ref: B2   Open: 7 days 12.00pm-2.00pm &
7.00pm-9.00pm

Tillmouth Park Country House Hotel

Cornhill-on-Tweed
01890 882255

Price £24

Tillmouth Park Hotel was built using stones from nearby Twizel Castle, which probably explains why the latter is now a ruin. The award-winning restaurant in the library on the first floor is the relaxed setting for an excellent meal with dishes typical of contemporary British cuisine. Terrine of local game, dressed salad and Cumberland sauce to start or Home-made salmon and coriander cakes with yoghurt dressing show the flair behind the dishes. Entrees like Grilled lamb cutlets with minted couscous or Tagliatelli with sweet peppers, white wine, garlic and cream, as a vegetarian option, continue the theme. Local cheeses with home-made chutney to finish or maybe the Bread and butter pudding with vanilla sauce. Coffee and a liqueur in one of the lounges will round everything off very nicely. Enjoy!

Map ref: B1   Open: 7 days 7.00pm-8.45pm,
Sun 12.00pm-1.45pm

Topsey Turvey's

2, Dial Place, **Warkworth**
01665 711338

Price £25

A warm, friendly atmosphere in this small restaurant where people chat across the tables and themed events are a speciality. Although small, the menu is anything but meagre and the servings are even bigger. The a la carte has 18 starters with delicious soups and seafood dishes. The lobsters and crabs are bought fresh off the boats in Amble and the venison comes from local farmers, so everything is very fresh. The Chicken Wellington served with one of four sauces is a feast in itself and one of my favourites, but it's hard to resist the fish, so you'll probably have to make a return visit. The call of the Seabass served with garlic prawns and the Char-grilled tuna steak served with Mediterranean vegetables is just too strong. The desserts are all home-made and it shows. The service is friendly; the chef often joins the diners at the end of the evening to chat and enjoy the company.

Open: Wed-Sat 10.30am-3.30pm;
Tues- Sat 7.00pm-late;
Sun 10.30am-4.00pm.

Map ref: C3

The Valley

The Old Station House, **Corbridge**
01434 633434

Price £20

The "world renowed Passage to India train service" offers customers of The Valley the chance of a whistle-stop, escorted journey from Newcastle to Corbridge and the station house setting of this unusual restaurant. In the dedicated carriage, the waiter in full Raj regalia serves your aperitifs as you trundle through the beautiful Tyne Valley. On arrival the accent is on immaculate service in very comfortable surroundings. In winter the open fireplace is the focal point of the cosy bar. The decor of yellows, creams and terracotta adds to the ambience. The menu carries a full range of curried dishes including some from Ceylon, which are cooked with strongly flavoured spices that make the food hotter but balanced with lots of coconut to temper the fire. There are several dishes unique to the chef. Attention to detail combined with excellent quality are the hallmarks of this restaurant.

Open: Mon-Sat 6.00pm-11.00pm

Map ref: B5

Valley Connection 301

Market Place, **Hexham**
01434 601234

Price £22

Overlooking the ancient market place in historic Hexham, Valley Connection is the latest addition to the award-winning Valley group of restaurants. Lemon and terracotta decor with blond, bentwood chairs, diffused and sculpted lighting spilling through a balconied opening from the upper dining room to the floor below. The menu has a broad range of dishes with some special to this particular one. A glossary of spices enhances diners' appreciation of the craft behind each dish. Belati Baigon Zhal Zul (king prawns prepared with fresh tomatoes, green chillis and fresh coriander) has a creamy consistency and a tangy flavour. For those who want a more challenging experience, the chef offers more fiery curries ranging from madras through to vindaloo which, surprisingly, owes its name to early Portuguese settlers. You learn something every day.

Map ref: B5   Open: Tues-Sun 6.00pm-11.00pm

The Victoria Hotel

Bamburgh
01668 214431

Price £25

The Victoria Hotel overlooks the village green, just a stone's throw from the imposing Bamburgh Castle. The area is steeped in history but you step from the ancient into the modern when you enter the award-winning brasserie. The dining room has an al fresco feel, set in a glass roofed courtyard with warm, terracotta walls and stylish artwork. The chefs present an equally stylish menu using local delicacies to make dishes like Seahouse smoked haddock fishcakes with green salad and salsa vierge and Tian of Farne Island crab with tiger prawns, mixed leaves and black olive tapenade. Entrées are just as enticing. Cassoulet of giant Greek beans with plum tomatoes, fresh herbs and glazed with halloumi cheese or Pan-fried Bamburg sausages with aioli mash and a carbonnade of onions. Try the "Vic's" own bread and butter pudding with sauce Anglaise to finish or the Pear and frangipan tart with gin and lavender ice cream. Now there's a challenge.

Map ref: C2   Open: 7 days 7.00pm-9.00pm
last orders;
Sun 12.00pm-3.00pm

Northumberland tea rooms

*THE BARK POTS
9 West End, Craster
Tel: (01665) 576286 www.barkpots.co.uk
Open daily from 10am-4pm
This family run tea room offers traditional home-baking and world famous Craster Kippers. It is located one mile from Dunstanburgh Castle and picnic packs are made to order.
Map ref: C2

*BROCKBUSHES FARM SHOP & TEA ROOM
Stocksfield, Corbridge
Tel: (01434) 633100 www.brockbushes.co.uk
Open 10am-5.30pm
Corbridge is a pretty village with lots of speciality gift shops. This tea room forms part of Brockbushes Farm Shop which stocks home-made cakes, quiches, savoury pies and tempting desserts, many of which are on the menu. You can also pick your own fruit available in season.
Map ref: B5

*THE BYRE TEA ROOM
Harbottle
Tel: (01669) 650476 www.the-byre.co.uk
Open weekends/public holidays 11am-5pm
This tea room is located in a beautiful farm byre and offers home-baked cakes and 'singin' hinnies' griddled while you wait. Home-made sandwiches are also made to order including a good vegan selection.
Map ref: B3

*THE CAFE AT BRADLEY GARDENS
Sled Lane, Wylam
Tel: (01661) 852176 www.bradleygardens.co.uk
Open 10am-4.30pm daily
The cafe is situated within a large Edwardian conservatory overlooking beautiful gardens. Specialities on the menu include home-cooked soup and Panini, blueberry toffee crunch cake and chocolate brownies to die for. There is also a fine selection of plants, shrubs and herbs on sale.
Map ref: C4

CHADWICKS
26 Middle Street, Corbridge
Tel: (01434) 632429
Open 9am-5pm Monday to Saturday
Situated in the attractive old village of Corbridge, this tea room has monthly events serving specialities including fruity Moroccan lamb, grilled salmon with pesto and Parmesan crust and wholemeal carrot cake.
Map ref: B5

CORNMILL COFFEE SHOP
19 St Mary's Chare, Hexham
Tel: (01434) 601577
Open 9.30pm - 5pm Monday to Saturday
Located in the heart of the historic market town of Hexham, this coffee shop is located within a building housing a gift and craft shop and holistic therapy centre. The menu features a good selection of vegetarian food.
Map ref: B5

*DOXFORD COUNTRY STORE
Doxford Farm
Tel: (01665) 579477
www.doxfordfarmcottages.com
Open 10am-5pm daily
You will find this tea room within a farm courtyard along with gift shop, clothes shop and art gallery. It is near to a farm walk and holiday cottages making it an excellent place to finish off your walk.
Map ref: C2

FOUNTAIN COTTAGE TEAROOMS
Council Offices, Bellingham
Tel:(1434) 220172
Open Tuesday-Sunday 10am-4pm and open on bank holiday Mondays
On the banks of the North Tyne, Bellingham offers wild and uncompromising countryside along with a warm welcome. This tea room is housed within the same building as the Tourist Information Centre, near to a lovely walk up to Hareshaw Linn and on route to Kielder. Serves all home-made food and cakes.
Map ref: B4

THE GREENHOUSE
21 Dial Place, Warkworth
Tel: (01665) 712322
Open weekdays 9-4pm (winter) and Thursday, Friday and Saturday evenings
Located in the pretty village of Warkworth, near to the Castle and other local attractions, the menu at this tea room serves a good wholesome selection of home-baked food.
Map ref: C3

THE HEMMEL COFFEE SHOP
Heritage Centre, Allenheads, Hexham
Tel: (01434) 685395
Open 10am-5pm daily (seasonal opening times may vary)
Close to the Heritage Centre, blacksmiths shop, engine house and lovely nature trail, the specialities on this menu at this coffee shop include home-made soups, healthy salads and very popular carrot cake.
Map ref: B5

* Northumbria Tourist Board member

HEXHAM TANS TEA ROOM & RESTAURANT
11 St Mary's Chare, Hexham
Tel: (01434) 656284
Open 8.30am- 4pm - Tuesday to Saturday
Close to the Abbey, Old Gaol and historic market town of Hexham, the menu at this tea room is totally vegetarian and vegans are catered for. All food is fresh and home-made on the premises. Famous for wholemeal cheese and fruit scones.
Map ref: B5

THE IMPROMPTU CAFE
The Schoolhouse, Elsdon
Tel: (01830) 520389
Open 10am-5pm daily (seasonal opening times may differ)
Serving a delicious selection of home-made food including old-fashioned soup and apple pie, this café is located three miles from Otterburn, near to the Pele Tower and gibbet dating back to 1791. It's ideal for cyclists and walkers and is a National Park Information Point.
Map ref: B3

LAUNDRY COURT COFFEE HOUSE
Kirkharle Courtyard, Kirkharle
Tel: (01830) 540426
Open 10am-5pm daily
This tea room is located within a Georgian courtyard with many attractions including an exhibition about Capability Brown (a 17th century garden designer), photographic gallery, sculptor, cabinet maker, speciality food shop, bicycle museum plus a large working model railway.
Map ref: B4

*MILLFIELD COUNTRY CAFE
Main Road, Millfield, Wooler
Tel: 01668 216323
Open Monday to Saturday 8am-6pm, Sunday 9am-7pm
Serving delicious pastries, cakes and freshly cooked meals, this café is near to a small craft shop and the National Park & Maelmin Heritage Trail Information Point - ideal for ramblers.
Map ref: B2

MRS MIGGINS COFFEE HOUSE
9 The Granary, St Mary's Wynd, Hexham
Tel: (01434) 605808
Open 9am-5pm Monday to Saturday
This tea room is handy for Hexham town centre, the Abbey and market place (open Friday, Saturday and Tuesday). It serves light lunches and you could try a Mrs Miggins mega sandwich if you're very hungry.
Map ref: B5

*OXFORD FARM SHOP AND TEA ROOM
Ancroft
Tel: (01289) 387253 www.oxfordfarmshop.co.uk
Open 10am-7pm daily except for Mondays
This traditional farmhouse tea room serves specialities including preserves, jams and home-made meringues. You can pick your own strawberries when in season and coarse fishing is available at the farm.
Map ref: B1

*NORTHUMBERLAND CHEESE COFFEE SHOP
Make me Rich Farm, Blagdon
Tel: (01670) 789798
www.northumberland-cheese.co.uk
Open daily 10am-5pm
This tea room is located within a Northumberland dairy where you can see how cheeses are made in the traditional way and sample the delights of an interesting menu, which includes fabulous cheese soup and scones - all made on site.
Map ref: C4

PEBBLES
Shield Street, Allendale
Tel: (01434) 683975
Open 10am-4.30pm Tuesday to Sunday plus bank holidays. Also open for evening meals on Fridays and Saturdays.
The tea room is located in Allendale, a village surrounded by moorland which stands 1,400 ft above sea level. They serve speciality teas and coffees and home-cooked food using local, fresh ingredients.
Map ref: B5

PHAT KATZ
The Old Grammar School Stables, Hexham
Tel: (01434) 606656
Open 9.30am-5pm Monday to Saturday
Situated in the centre of Hexham, near to the Old Gaol and Hexham Abbey this coffee shop displays an unusual collection of memorabilia from the local area and serves delicious home-made cakes and scones.
Map ref: B5

*ROCK MIDSTEAD ORGANIC FARM SHOP AND TEAROOM
Rock Midstead, Alnwick, Northumberland
Tel: (01665) 579225
Open 10am-5pm daily (except for Mondays in winter).
This tea room offers light lunches and afternoon teas and caters well for vegetarians and special diets ie gluten free meals. It is located five miles from Alnwick.
Map ref: C2

* Northumbria Tourist Board member

*ROSEDEN FARM SHOP
Wooperton, Alnwick
Tel: (01668) 217271 www.roseden.com
Open Tuesday to Saturday 10am-5pm (and on Sundays in the summer)
This tea room and traditional farm shop offers an excellent selection of home produce and a range of local gifts.
Map ref: C2

SCHOOL ROOM TEAS
Matfen
Tel: (01661) 886202
Open 10am-5pm April to October.
This tea room is located within Matfen Village Store (which is a shop and post office) and is a must for cyclists on the Rievers coast to coast cycle route. The special cyclists menu includes a bowl of soup, sandwich and slice of cake. It is situated in the picturesque village of Matfen, six miles from Corbridge.
Map ref: B4

SIMONBURN TEA ROOMS
1 The Mains, Simonburn
Tel: (01434) 681321
Open daily 10am-5pm
Simonburn is a small hamlet near to Hadrians Wall that has featured in several Catherine Cookson TV films. This tea room is situated within a 19th century shop and is also near to the 13th century church of St Mungo. This used to be the biggest parish in the country.
Map ref: B4

THORTERGILL TEA ROOMS
Thortergill, Garrigill, Alston, Cumbria
Tel: (01434)381936 www.thortergillforge.com
Open March to November 10am-5pm Tuesday to Sunday and Bank holiday Mondays
Thortergill is a wooded gorge, which has been restored to its pre-lead mining condition. You can walk up the gorge to the waterfall or watch the blacksmiths at work. The tea room serves lunches, soups, pies and gluten-free cake. It's located on the borders of Durham, Cumbria and Northumberland.
Map ref: A5

*WATERSIDE TEA ROOMS
Bavington Hall, Little Bavington,
Tel: (01830) 530394 www.bavingtonhall.co.uk
Open 10am-5pm daily
This tea room is located within the 13th century Bavington Hall, surrounded by beautiful restored gardens. Specialities include home-cooked scones and cakes with afternoon tea. You can enjoy the waterside setting and some peace and tranquility within the gardens and there's also a golf buggy on site for customers to use.
Map ref: B4

*WEAVERS COFFEE SHOP
Otterburn Mill, Otterburn
Tel: (01830) 520225 www.otterburnmill.co.uk
Open 10am-4pm daily
For a taste of traditional Northumbrian industry try a visit to Otterburn, home of a former 17th century mill that used to create world-famous tweeds and woollens. The mill is no longer in operation but is open to the public to sell Otterburn Tweeds. The coffee shop is located within the mill that also houses an exhibition and mill shop.
Map ref: B3

WHITE MONK TEA ROOM
The Square, Blanchland
Tel: (01434) 675233
Open daily 10.30am - 5pm June to September plus weekends from March-May and October. Blanchland, close to the Derwent Reservoir, is considered to be one of England's most beautiful villages. This tea room is located near to the main square in the village, which dates back to the 12th century. Specialities include home-made jams, chutneys, cakes and traditional afternoon tea.
Map ref: B5

* Northumbria Tourist Board member

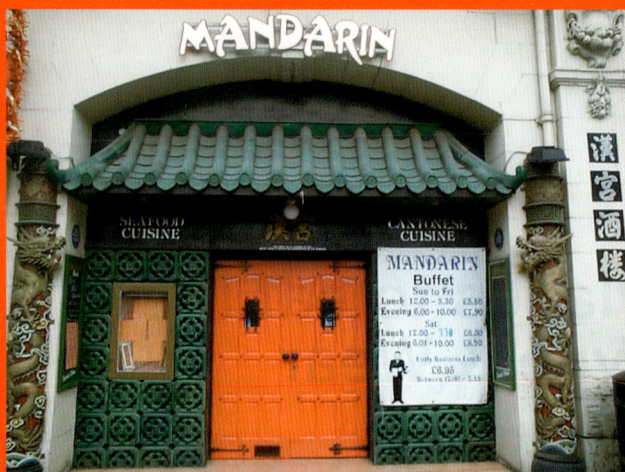
44

Tyne & Wear map

A   B   C

Seaton Burn
A1 Gosforth Park Shiremoor Whitley Bay
1   1
A696 Forest Hall A19
                          Tynemouth
      Gosforth   North
                     Shields South
      Jesmond   Shields

Newcastle
upon Tyne   Heaton   Jarrow   Whitburn

TYNE &
WEAR   Gateshead   East Boldon
2   2

Gibside   A1 Washington
                          Sunderland

                    A19

3   3
              Houghton
              le Spring

A   B   C

Bazil Brasserie

South Parade
Whitley Bay
0191 293 9898

A New Continental style restaurant where diners can enjoy fine wines and great food in comfortable, contemporary surroundings.

Bazil is one of the first restaurants in the region to gain an RAC Blue Ribbon award for dining excellence.

A la Carte menu changes with the seasons, chef specials blackboard changes daily.

Starters from £3.50
Main dishes from £7.95

11 Tavistock Place

11, Tavistock Place, **Sunderland**
0191 514 5000

Price £30

Tavistock Place has earned a reputation for being innovative - and change keeps on rolling on. The restaurant now boasts the largest private collection of famous faces in the North-East. Pictures of glittering literati and sparkling film stars are everywhere. It's the one place where you can sit next to Sophia Loren or rub shoulders with John Wayne as you enjoy the delicious food on offer. Starters like Pressed duck and foie gras terrine with a Madeira jelly lead on to entrées such as Crusted cannon of pork with crushed potatoes, rhubarb and ginger sauce or Beetroot and ricotta ravioli, rocket pesto and parmesan wafers. So imaginative. Desserts continue the theme with Pink peppercorn meringue with black treacle ice cream and Hot chocolate pudding with coconut sorbet. All this and Margot Fonteyn's ballet shoes too! Check out the lunchtime and evening blackboard specials.

Open: Mon-Fri 12.00pm-2.00pm last orders & 6.00pm-10.00pm last orders; Sat 12.00pm-2.00pm last orders & 7.00pm-10.00pm

Map ref: C2

Ahad

78, High Street, **Gosforth**
0191 284 4088

Price £24

Stylish comfort with modern decor, muslin drapes and muted lighting. A family business run by four brothers as part of group of fashionable restaurants in the city. A traditional menu with its own secret recipes like Salmon Ahad and the chicken dish, Puttley Murgh. They are more open about the Chicken [or lamb] with lemongrass, which is a house speciality and the Jhinga Lajawab (king sized prawns stir fried with spices and onions) - recommended as star dishes. Tucked away behind the High Street, popular with locals who keep coming back. This is a very attractive restaurant in look and feel and worth a visit.

Open: Mon-Sat 12.00pm-2.00pm; Mon-Thurs 6.00pm-11.30pm; Fri-Sat 6.00pm -12.00am; Sun 6.30-11.30pm

Map ref:B1

Amici

95, Station Road, **Forest Hall**
0191 215 1115

Price £24

Spacious, airy and very stylish: lavender, terracotta and burnt red walls, muslin draping the windows and sprays of lights. Amici offers a modern and Mediterranean menu with a generous range of blackboard specials. There are so many attractive features to this restaurant that it is usually full to bursting. The lunchtime and early bird menu for £4.50 is such good value that the punters swarm in, in droves. For those with a little more money to spend the a la carte offers a smooth Chicken liver paté with Cumberland sauce while the blackboard has King prawns in chilli, tomato and cream sauce. Main courses, Salmon with Hollandaise sauce or Roasted lamb fillet in red wine and garlic, come with hefty servings of chips.The desserts are tempting. Like all good restaurants, it appeals to the eye as well as the tastebuds.

Map ref: B1

Open: Mon-Sat 12.00pm-2.30pm & 5.30pm-10.30pm; Sun 12.00pm-2.30pm & 6.00pm-10.00pm

Arlecchino

208, Heaton Road, **Heaton**
0191 265 0044

Price £20

The harlequin theme runs throughout, from the dazzling diamond exterior to the clowns, masquerade murals and pierrots inside. The affable owner creates a welcoming atmosphere to this well-established family-run restaurant. Soft background jazz and occasional live music nights make this a restaurant with an artistic difference. Pizzas and pastas are there but the menu offers much more. Dishes like Cacio di capra (warm goat-cheese, pimentos, olives and salad), Honey roast duck with spice, cassis and port sauce, and Partridge casserole with root vegetables and wine. Local cheeses like Apricot with stilton are a speciality as is the exceptionally fine cellar with wines imported directly from Italy. Pavement tables in summer add to the continental feel.

Map ref: B2

Open: 7 days 12.00-2.00pm & 5.00-11.00 pm

Barn Again Bistro

21a Leazes Park Road, **Newcastle**
0191 230 3338

Price £28

Barn Again is one of Newcastle's more relaxed restaurants with its jumble of mismatched tables and chairs and informal atmosphere. Very popular with the young and young at heart. En route to St James's Park, Magpie fans can get a special lunch-time meal if they book in advance. Dishes like Pan-fried chicken livers with ciabatta, avocado puree, hazelnuts and kumquat relish (£6) with Cod fillet seared with smoked paprika, red peppers, green lentils and spicy almond pesto (£13) are part of the pan global range with something to tempt every palate. Presentation is their strong suit with each dish accompanied by a flourish of garnish and a good humoured waiter.

Open: Mon- Fri 12.00pm- 2.00pm; Mon-Sat 6.30pm-10.00pm

Map ref: B2

Bay's Bistro

183, Park View, **Whitley Bay**
0191 251 3567

Price £25

The warm, relaxed interior is full of interesting, quirky objets d'art. The humour in the decor is reflected in the menu with dishes like Off the cuff soup and goes on to offer a range from around the world. How about the Roast pork fillet wrapped in air dried ham, spicy charkalaka mango, lime and honey salsa, crispy shallots or Lime, coriander and chilli chicken baked in Chinese pastry, fried yams, sweet and sour sauce. The desserts are just as imaginative and enticing. The friendly atmosphere, weekday specials and unusual menu have made this a very popular restaurant.

Open: Tues- Sat 5.00pm- 10.00pm; Sun 12.00pm- 2.30pm

Map ref: C1

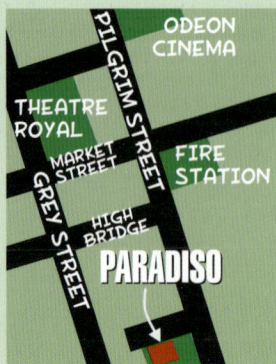

Bazil Brasserie

South Parade, **Whitley Bay**
0191 293 9898

Price £25

Bazil has got to be the most stylish restaurant in Whitley Bay. Set on the lively nightclub/bar strip of this bustling seaside town, with interior design of deep blues, gleaming silver and mellow beech wood - it's very chic. The menu is highly contemporary: featherlight Crab spring roll with a sweet chilli dipping sauce or seductive Sautéed chicken livers flambéed with brandy, served on a toasted brioche, and that's just the starters. The Poached chicken breast stuffed with mozzarella and basil is a succulent treat, but then there is always the delicate charms of the Grilled salmon with wilted greens and wild mushrooms. Save some space for the desserts; Summer berry pavlova for a light finish or the Duo of chocolate torte for the more robust appetite. Whatever you choose, a meal at this award-winning restaurant will be one to remember.

Open: Mon-Sat 5.30pm-10.00pm;
Sun 12.00pm-3.00pm & 7.00pm-
10.00pm

Map ref: C1

Big Mussel

15, The Side, **Newcastle**
0191 232 1057

Price £35

Handily situated on the busy route to the Quayside, Big Mussel appeals to those out for something a little different. The style is casual with pale wooden seats and a silver balustrade along the unusual first floor balcony. As you would expect mussels and fish feature prominently with fourteen ways to order mussels alone. But if you do fancy meat you can to choose from a range of steak and chicken dishes. You might like to start with King prawn tropicana, prawns coated in breadcrumbs and coconut with a spicy tomato salsa. Then for a main course how about Waterzooi, a traditional Belgian fish casserole of mussels, salmon, scallops, potato and mushrooms. which you can wash down with one or more of a large selection of Belgian beers. There are some special offers such as the intriguing Clock-saver where from 5.30pm to 7.00pm the time you order is the price you pay, ie. if you order at 5.40pm you pay £5.40. The early bird catches the mussel!

Open: Mon-Sat 12.00pm-2.00pm
& 5.30pm-10.00pm;
Sun 5.30 pm-10.00pm.

Map ref: B2

Blackfriars Café Bar

Friar Street, **Newcastle**
0191 261 5945

Price £27

Situated in a 13th century Dominican refectory, Blackfriars is the oldest restaurant in the country - but the menu is definitely 21st century. The interior is an eclectic mix of modern retro with a collection of mis-matched tables and chairs that add to the atmosphere of the bistro-style restaurant. The lunch-time menu has a range of light dishes with pitta pockets and tortilla wraps, salads and a scattering of desserts. Dinner is a more substantial affair with aperitifs followed by Thai crab salad with Asian coleslaw to start and Red mullet, mussel, saffron and fennel broth with aioli and garlic bread to follow. The robust diner can tangle with the Lamb kofta with yoghurt raita and pitta strips followed by Seared rib-eye steak on Caesar salad, anchovies and parmesan shavings. Desserts are delicious and the setting and service makes this a must on the historic tour.

Map ref: B2   *Open: Tues-Sun 12.00pm-2.30pm*
Wed-Sat 6.00pm-10.00pm

Blakes Coffee House

53, Grey Street, **Newcastle**
0191 261 5463

Price £10

A walk-in welcome to this super-lively cafe, the closely packed tables mean that it's shoulder-to-shoulder eating. Customers can request their favourite CDs and sometimes the jukebox is brought into service. Legend has it that a stone mason died in the construction of this listed building and his mates carved his face into a cornerstone. He peers out dolefully, head held in his hands, watching the customers enjoy a variety of hot and cold dishes (Lasagne, Chilli, Cumberland sausage and mash), sandwiches and baguettes, cakes and pastries. You can choose any combination from 600 sandwich fillings, the strangest one so far being chicken, Brie and strawberries, only topped by the person who ordered mayonnaise with her cheesecake - all provided with the same cheery smile.

Map ref: B2   *Open: Mon-Fri 7.00am-6.00pm*
Sat 7.30am-5.30pm
Sun 10.00pm-4.00pm

Buon Appetito

6, Salters Road, **Gosforth**
0191 213 6401

Price £25

From the minute you step through the door into the welcoming bar area you are struck by the friendly, easy going atmosphere of this place. Always busy, and with good cause, this is the place for a relaxed, after-work meal or a more leisurely dinner. The menu is mainly Italian but, with home-made pasta, the accent is on quality - and it shows. Side-stepping the obligatory pizza-pasta dishes (which are good), there are plenty of Pollo dishes like the Siciliana, chargrilled chicken breast with king prawns, lime, garlic and white wine. If you prefer lamb you could try the Agnellino al rosemarino, chargrilled rack of lamb with shallots, rosemary, garlic and red wine. Desserts galore to round off the meal and a good range of robust wines from the regions make this a very attractive venue.

Open: Mon-Sat 12.00pm-2.30pm;
Mon-Wed 5.30pm-10.00pm;
Thurs-Sat 5.30pm-10.30pm

Map ref: B1

Café 21

21, Queen Street, **Newcastle**
0191 222 0755

Price £25

This very stylish brasserie is the flagship of Terry Laybourne's fleet of restaurants - and is one of the finest in town. The service is very professional - always on hand but so discreet. The modern, clean lines of the interior provide an informal backdrop to a splendid menu. As a starter Laybourne's signature dish of Cheddar cheese and spinach souffle is a must. The menu descriptions understate the artistry clearly apparent in each dish. Don't be fooled by the ordinary-sounding Fish, chips and mushy peas - nothing is as simple as it seems. The desserts are fabulous. If you tire of eating here you're tired of life!

Open: Mon-Sat 12.00 pm-2.00 pm
& 6.00 pm-10.30 pm

Map ref: B2

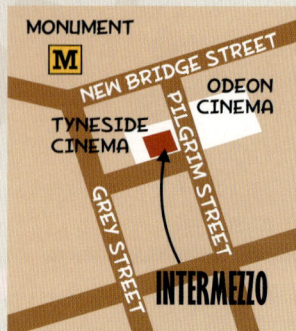

Café in the Garden

Eldon Garden, Newcastle
0191 221 1511

Price £17

The setting presents as an oasis of calm amidst the hurly burly of the shopping malls. Glass-domes, open and airy, put down your bags, take the weight off your feet and enjoy the space. Home-cooked scones the size of cushions, breakfast and brunch meals to satisfy the hungry shopper and deli specials provide a good range of light meals. Blackboard specials like Moules Mariniere, Chilli con carne, Lasagna and a range of salads provide more substantial meals. Everything is cooked to order. Stop here and take stock before you set off again in search of retail heaven.

Open: Mon-Fri 9.00am-5.30pm; Thurs 9.00am-8.00pm; Sat

Map ref: B2

Café Indigo

Kenilworth Hotel, Osborne Road, Jesmond
0191 281 9111

Price £25

The Osborne Road strip is buzzing with restaurants and bars. The first surprise with Indigo is that the interior is red - not a hint of purple anywhere. The general look of the place is moody and quietly jazzy. Scattered pictures and dimmed shell wall-lights, wooden floors and tables, stylish tableware - everything to relax the Jesmond parents and affluent youngies that fill the restaurant. The menu is just as designer aware. Thai fishcakes with shiracha or Grilled skewered chicken with spicy peanut sauce as starters, followed by Black bream topped with ginger and lemongrass crust with oriental stir-fried noodles or Jamaican chicken sweet potato and plantain mash with an allspice pineapple sauce. Very exotic. There is a full range of desserts, something to please everyone.

Open: Mon -Sat 12.00pm-2.00pm & 5.30pm-10.30pm; Sun 12.00pm-9.30pm.

Map ref: B1

Café Neon

8, Bigg Market, **Newcastle**
0191 260 2577

Price £12

Continental menu, a light and breezy cafe bar in the Bigg Market, a popular lunchtime venue for office workers. Ground floor the atmosphere is busy with loud music and the cabaret of an open kitchen area. Down the spiral staircase and you are in an altogether quieter, more intimate room. Gently lit alcoves and screened corners, plus the imaginative use of tapestries and rugs as wall-hangings create a Mediterranean feel without insisting on a holiday mood. You can get anything from an all-day breakfast to hot baguettes, toasties, omelettes and pasta dishes. It is one of a burgeoning number of cafes that provide pavement tables so that customers can eat al fresco. Students and regulars enjoy a 10% discount.

Open: Mon-Sat 10.00am-6.00pm   Map ref: B2

Casa del Sol

37, Pink Lane, **Newcastle**
0191 221 0122

Price £16

First of a number of tapas bars in Newcastle, the poster-papered walls and Iberian ephemera firmly fix the Latin character. Meats, cheeses and wines imported from Spain add to the authenticity of the dishes. Special events like Flamenco evenings and regional Spanish wine tasting with appropriate food are additional attractions. Local game features strongly on the daily blackboard specials. All these elements make this a restaurant with a difference. There are good value midweek specials, Tuesday - Thursday, from 6.30 - 9.30pm when £15.99 will get two people a choice of four tapas dishes and a jug of Sangria. Bring your own castanets!

Open: Tues - Sat 6.30 - 11.30 pm.   Map ref:B2

Centurion Bar and Brasserie

Central Station, Neville Street, **Newcastle**
0191 230 2714

Price £25

The Centurion is a series of surprises. First is the beautifully-tiled Victorian bar café area, very popular for lunches and an after-work drink. Going through to the brasserie leaves all the busy-ness of the street and station behind and takes you into a world of calm chic, with candle-lit pre-dinner sofas and rattan chairs, on to the dining rooms with their honey wood tables and floors, curved leather seating and so relaxed atmosphere. The menu leads you on further into the evening with Spiced duck terrine with caramelised orange dressing or Game sausage, parsnip mash and crispy onions. Entrées like Ginger spiced pork fillet with sweet potato mash and five spice syrup or Wok fried bak choi, wild mushroom with lemongrass and chilli rice precede desserts such as Bakewell tart with vanilla ice cream or Northumbrian cheese and biscuits. A super setting for a wonderful meal.

Map ref: B2   *Open: Mon-Sat 7.00pm-late*

Copthorne Hotel - Harry's Bar & Restaurant

The Close, Quayside, **Newcastle**
0191 222 0333

Price £24

Harry's bar and restaurant is named after the famous Tyneside rower Harry Clasper. A waterside theme runs through from the oars in reception to the fishes on the carpet. A light airy informal atmosphere. Floor to ceiling windows open onto the tree-lined riverside terrace for those warmer evenings or even a bracing breakfast. Sandwiches and snacks are served all day. Family groups are welcome and the chef will provide any variation of menu dishes to tempt the youngest palate and avoid tantrums over unwanted sprouts. Try the Roasted artichoke and sun dried vegetables glazed with chevere goats cheese, for a starter, followed by Stir fried prawns and blackbean sauce with rice and crispy noodles. For dessert, Pear and almond tart served with creme fraiche.

Map ref: B2   *Open: Sun- Fri 12.00pm-2.30pm*
                   & Sun-Sat 7.00pm-10.00pm

Copthorne Hotel - Le Rivage

The Close, Quayside, **Newcastle**
0191 222 0333

Price £40

Leading through from Harry's, a more formal, intimate restaurant for luxury dining. Cream, gold and deep blue, subtle lighting and silver service. Enjoy your apperitifs on the pre-dinner sofas in its own bar followed by appetisers: Smoked duck and chicken with an avocado salad and a pink peppercorn dressing or Fresh mussels in a Thai green curry sauce. Classic main courses with a twist include Medallions of beef with smoked bacon and asparagus in a rich Rioja jus and Aubergine gateau with creamed leeks, cherry tomatoes and wild mushrooms. The desserts are deliciously recognisable favourites. The perfect end to a riverside stroll.

Open: Mon- Sat 7.30pm-9.30pm   Map ref: B2

Da Vinci's

73 Osborne Road, **Jesmond**
0191 281 5284

Price £34

Even though there has been a surge of new restaurants popping up on all sides, the long established Da Vinci's has retained it's classic, stylish elegance. It offers Italian cuisine with a wide selection of dishes based on traditional recipes. The chef enjoys cooking fish, which he collects daily from the quay and his chicken dishes are very popular. The owners make trips to Italy several times a year to stock the wine cellar in order to provide a bottle to suit everybody's pocket. Haute cuisine at affordable prices.

Open: 7 days 12.00pm-2.30pm;   Map ref: B1
Sun-Thurs 5.30pm-10.30pm;
Fri-Sat 5.30pm-11.00pm

Daraz Tandoori Restaurant

4 Holly Avenue West, **Jesmond**
0191 281 8431

Price £2

Daraz is Jesmond's oldest Indian restaurant. It has survived this long because of the quality of the food. However, in keeping with trends in the area, it now boasts clean, pale yellow walls, subtle lighting, crisp linen and an air of bustling newness. The restaurant specialises in Bangladeshi cuisine, with traditional recipes of the region and fresh herbs and spices bringing the character of the dishes to life. As well as the more usual main courses there is a long list of chef's specialities, mostly priced at £8.95. The set meal for two (£34.95) is good value and, if you can't make it there, they'll deliver to you. How obliging.

Map ref:B1

Open: Mon-Sat 12.00pm-2.00pm
& 5.30pm-12.30am
Sun 6.00pm-11.30pm

Don Vito's

82, Pilgrim Street, **Newcastle**
0191 232 8923

Price £2

Established in 1976 this popular city centre restaurant is well situated for that after-the-shops meal or a pre-theatre dinner. It has a bustling, friendly cafe style. If you are looking for somewhere that is a bit different to the other Italian restaurants in town, without it hitting your pocket too hard, look no further. Try the Polpettine al sugo (that's meatballs in tomato sauce to you!) as a starter and follow that with a robust pasta dish or, for the more adventurous among you, the Merluzzo con insalata di fagioli (chunky Atlantic cod with black olive pesto and a warm white bean salad). A variety of breads are baked daily on the premises.

Map ref: B2

Open: Mon-Fri 12.00pm-2.00pm
& 5.00pm-10.00pm
Sat 11.45am-10.30pm

Dragon House

30-32, Stowell Street, **Newcastle**
0191 232 0868

rice £23

Plush surroundings and subtle lighting make the most of the blue and gold interior. Like its sister restaurants along Stowell Street, the Dragon House offers a range of set meals to guide the less adventurous through the vast number of dishes on offer. The difference here is that their menus include some rather innovative and surprising items. Da Da chicken, strips of marinaded chicken in an oyster sauce and stir-fried, Oyster and roast pork hot pot, similarly marinaded and baked slowly in a hot pot and don't go without trying the Scallops served in birds nest. Several twists on the Cantonese theme.

pen: 7 days 12.00pm-2.00pm & .00pm-11.30pm

Map ref: B2

Eslington Villa

8, Station Road, Low Fell, **Gateshead**
0191 487 6017

rice £27

A large, Victorian house tucked away in a secluded corner of Gateshead, serving very good food at reasonable prices. Country house chic with modern flourishes and a popular lunch venue for local business people. Their reputation for artistic, contemporary cuisine is supported by their ability to attract the region's top chefs. They are passionate about food. Salad of crab and avocado with grapefruit dressing followed by Saddle of rabbit with fresh pasta, slow roast tomatoes and garlic butter and, to round off, Nougat glace with fresh raspberries. Tempted? Give in and go.

Open: Mon-Fri 12.00 pm-2.00 pm; un 12.00 pm-3.00 pm; Mon-Sat 7.00 pm-10.00 pm

Map ref: B2

The only Thai restaurant in Newcastle City Centre

Thai Siam

Authentic Thai cuisine
Traditional Thai surroundings

Exquisite seafood
Fully licensed
Vegetarian
Air conditioned
80 seat cover

16 Stowell Street
Newcastle upon Tyne
(China Town)
Reservations:
0191 232 0261

OPENING HOURS

MONDAY - SATURDAY
Lunch 12noon - 2.15pm
Evening 6.00pm - 11.15pm

SUNDAY Evening 6.00pm - 11.00pm

Est Est Est

Quayside, **Newcastle**
0191 260 2291

*rice £24

An ultra-modern, open space of glass, chrome and blue light with lively music. This very stylish, riverside restaurant is a triumph of interior design, for those who like to be seen eating out. The waiters are business-like but the service is not always speedy, so be prepared to wait because on popular nights it is very, very busy. The menu is extensive with imaginative variations on the staple pizza-pasta dishes. It comes out with a creditable reputation for a lively meal out at a reasonable price.

Open: 7 days 12.00 pm 'til late   *Map ref: B2*

Fisherman's Lodge

Jesmond Dene, **Newcastle**
0191 281 3281

*rice £50

Deep within the landscaped luxury of Jesmond Dene, this recently refurbished restaurant offers chic dining in a pocket of urban countryisde. The menu is equally stylish but pricey. A three course set dinner without wine will set you back £34.50, but don't be put off because the food is excellent. Seared squid with courgette, garlic and olive oil sits well next to Confit of duck leg, Chinese vegetables and plum sauce. To finish there is a tangy Lemon cake with lemon curd. Spoil yourself. You're worth it.

Open: Mon-Fri 12.00pm-2.00pm   *Map ref: B1*
& 7.00pm-11.00pm
Sat 7.00pm-11.00pm

Hanahana

45, Bath Lane, **Newcastle**
0191 222 0282

Price £21

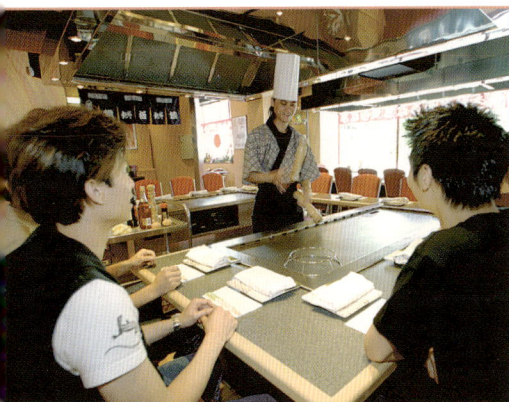

Part of the new wave of Japanese restaurants, Hanahana brings a spicy slice of the Orient to Newcastle. Each diner is welcomed with a resounding bash on the gong and a cheery greeting. The menu offers tappan yaki and sushi dishes with all the flash and flourish of cabaret cooking. Diners choose the raw ingredients (and accompanying sauces) which are then seared, flipped and flambéed on steel hot plates as you watch. Alongside the guided tour, banquet menus you can choose freely from the a la carte, makimono and moriwase dishes. Exotica such as Ika yaki, grilled calamari with Japanese hot sauce and Niku-gyoza, pan fried dumplings with chilli, sesame oil, vinegar and soya sauce dips lead on to every fish, meat and vegetable combination you can imagine cooked before you. As you would expect, everything is super-fresh and it's a highly entertaining way to eat out.

Open: Mon-Sat 6.00pm-11.00pm;
Sun-Sat 12.00pm-2.00pm;
Sun 6.00pm-10.30pm

Map ref: B2

Heartbreak Soup

77, Quayside, **Newcastle**
0191 222 1701

Price £22

The Quayside has caught up with Heartbreak Soup and it's holding its own. A laid-back, jazzy bistro atmosphere with a frieze of distinctive murals: the whole place has a unique style. The menu has dishes from right around the world: aromatic chicken from Tunisia, teriyaki chicken with seaweed and sushi from Japan, Korean duck breast with orange scented sticky rice, banana leaves and kumquat chutney - oriental spice meets Mediterranean herbs. A trip around the world in one place. These highly imaginative dishes are the hallmark of the restaurant. The menu is also very vegetarian-friendly and there is an impressive wine cellar.

Open: Mon- Thurs12.00pm-2.00 pm
& 6.00pm-10.00 pm; Fri 12.00pm-
2.00 pm & 6.00pm-11.00pm;
Sat 6.00pm-11.00pm

Map ref:B2

Horton Grange

Seaton Burn, **Newcastle**
01661 860686

Price £40

Country-house chic in atmosphere and appearance, Horton Gange is a luxury hotel with an established reputation for excellent food. The glass-fronted dining room leads onto a Japanese veranda overlooking a water garden. The extensive menu offers an outstanding variety of dishes, all described in loving detail: Slivers of smoked chicken and mango with salad leaves tossed in a walnut oil dressing; clear your palate with a refreshing sorbet or light Cream of leek and blue cheese soup and savour the Salmon and scallops set on buttered spinach leaves with a champagne and chive cream. The meal is beautifully rounded off with any one of a number of indulgent desserts like Hot vanilla soufflé served with caramel ice cream and lemon sauce. From the canapes to the coffee this is a highly polished performance of haute cuisine.

Map ref: B1   Open: Mon- Sat 7.00pm-8.45pm
                                       last orders

King Neptune

34-36 Stowell Street, **Newcastle**
0191 261 6657

Price £25

A highly acclaimed restaurant, the King Neptune has earned itself a place in the Egon Ronay guide for several years and continues to demonstrate a high standard of cooking and presentation. The traditional rich red and gold dining room downstairs strikes a contrast with the more modern lavender-blue room above. The regular customers, and there are many, enjoy the seamless, efficient service, the hallmark of this family-friendly restaurant. They specialise in fish dishes but the menu also has plenty of choice for the meat-eater or vegetarian. Flexible opening times accommodate special events like hungry football fans from the nearby St James's Park.

Map ref: B2   Open: 7 days 12.00pm-2.00pm;
                          Mon- Fri 6.30 pm-10.45 pm;
                               Sat 6.00pm-11.30 pm

Kublai Khan

23-29 The Side, **Newcastle**
0191 221 2203

Price £13.50 (buffet plus wine)

A popular restaurant, especially at weekends, with parties out for the night, Quayside revellers and couples who want a good meal for a good price. The result is a place with a lively atmosphere where you can freely enjoy yourself. Design your own meal at the Mongolian buffet, where you make your choice from a broad range of raw ingredients, meat, fish, vegetables and sauces which are then hot-seared on the griddle as you watch. There are suggested combinations of spices, but have fun and invent your own. Alternatively you can help yourself to the hot Chinese buffet. All you can eat, from Tuesdays to Saturdays, will cost you £13.50 and on Sundays and Mondays, £9.90.

Open: 7 days 6.00pm-10.30pm   Map ref: B2

La Riviera

Pipewellgate, **Gateshead**
0191 477 7070

Price £26

The old police station on the south bank of the Tyne has been transformed into a pool of Mediterranean colour. La Riviera has all the style and standards of a sophisticated Italian restaurant with the relaxed atmosphere and unpretentious cuisine of a top quality bistro. The setting is perfect for riverside-terrace aperitifs followed by a meal in the Renaissance-theme dining room. Fish dishes feature strongly on the menu and monkfish, prawns, salmon and sea bass appear in a range of imaginative combinations. Lamb, steak and poultry are not forgotten. Everything has that Riviera flourish and the desserts are no exception.

Open: Mon-Fri 12.00pm-2.30pm: Map ref: B2
Mon-Thurs 6.00pm-10.00pm:
Fri & Sat 6.00pm- 10.30pm

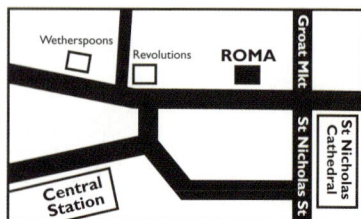

La Tasca

106, Quayside, **Newcastle**
0191 230 4006

Price £26 (tapas plus dessert)

One of a nationwide chain of tapas bars and restaurants, La Tasca has an unmistakably Spanish feel. Bold, earthy colours, dramatic lighting and splashes of colour in picture tiles, this large open place is filled with colour and joyful, vibrant salsa music. Not a place for a quiet conversation but great for a party meal, and there are party menus available. Six tapas dishes usually satisfies a couple of healthy appetites- choose from a gargantuan range guided by well-informed, friendly staff. Gambas, pollo and chorizo are all there or you can branch out and try a rustic Casserole of lamb with wine, onions, mustard and peppercorns. San Miguel beer or Rioja keep the Spanish theme going.

Open: Mon-Sat 12.00pm-11.00pm;
Sun 12.00pm-10.30pm   *Map ref: B2*

Lau's Buffet King

45-50 Stowell Street, **Newcastle**
0191 261 8868

Price: see text

An ultra-modern, cafeteria style, Lau's gives you fast food with taste. The place is always busily full of customers. You know the format: choose your food, eat as much as you want from the constantly replenished servery, and what you leave is cleared away, fast-food style. Choose any combination from the range of over 60 dishes: everything from Wan ton to Crispy duck to Sweet and sour somethings. Plenty of rice and noodles and a choice of fresh fruits and ice cream to follow. When I went there was hardly a chopstick in sight. The pricing system is somewhat complicated. The lunchtime price of £4.99 rises to £5.99 between 5.30-7.30 and £7.99 from then onwards. Great value for money. In addition, to entice you in, anyone over two years and under 4ft 11in eats for £2.99, no matter how big their appetite.

Open: 7 days 12.00pm-10.30pm   *Map ref: B2*

FISHERMAN'S LODGE

Newcastle's leading fish restaurant - in the heart of Jesmond Dene.

- Private dining • Day meetings
- Licensed for civil weddings.

Telephone (0191) 2813281

www.fishermanslodge.co.uk

Fisherman's Lodge Restaurant, Jesmond Dene, Newcastle upon Tyne, NE7 7BQ.

Fisherman's Lodge is one of Tom's Companies which also include Seaham Hall and Oriental Spa; The Samling and Treacle Moon Restaurant.

www.tomscompanies.com

Lucy's Italian Café

32, Clayton Street West, **Newcastle**
0191 261 0006

Price £23

Lucy's is on the edge of the party zone. The discreet facade belies the contemporary interior. The decor is warm, tasteful and humorous, with one room leading into another, the heart motif following as you go. The final surprise is the view of the trees (and garden) from the conservatory dining room. The full spectrum of standard Italian dishes from lasagne to linguine are here, but the difference between Lucy's and the bulk of the Italian restaurants is in the quality. Every dish is cooked with care, presented with flair and, consequently, eaten with relish. Recipes like Chicken liver and pistachio paté flavoured with brandy with red onion marmalade demonstrate the imagination behind the menu. For entrées: Roasted rack of lamb flavoured with rosemary and garlic and a fish dish, whose title goes on forever, which is Baked escalope of salmon rested on caramelised fennel and cordoned by a light dill sauce. Enough to make your mouth water. All this and desserts too.

Open: 7 days 10.00am-10.00pm   Map ref: B2

Malmaison Hotel Brasserie

104, The Close, **Newcastle**
0191 245 5001

Price £32

A richly dark interior with art deco curved, frosted glass panels screening dining booths and dramatic, wall-high prints; the Brasserie restaurant is redolent with French classic-contemporary style. Don't be put off by the imposing building, the atmosphere in the restaurant is relaxed and unaffected. There is a private dining room, seating up to 14, which boasts a wall of wine: bottles are used decoratively elsewhere. There is an eight-week rolling menu to reflect seasonal changes and a Carte Special which is the chef's decision of the day. The Sunday menu changes weekly. Start with Smoked haddock and saffron chowder with sweetcorn, diced potato pancetta; go on to Poulet bonne femme and indulge yourself with desserts like Chocolate delice or Cherry clafoutis.

Open: 7 days 12.00pm-2.30pm&   Map ref: B2
6.00pm-10.00pm

73

Mamma Mia's

46, Pudding Chare, **Newcastle**
0191 232 7193

Price £17

Celebrating 27 years in the business, Mamma Mia's is a friendly, typically Italian pizzeria just off the Bigg Market. Red gingham cloths, candles in Chianti bottles and walls covered in artistic graffiti set the scene. They profess a range of special dishes, several of which are not particularly Italian: Chicken wings in barbecue sauce, Beef stroganoff, Chicken Dijon and the like. A longstanding speciality is their rectangular pizza- the first cornered Capricciosa in town. The value-for-money lunchtime and early evening prices make it a popular venue.

Map ref: B2   Open: Mon-Sat 12.00pm-2.30pm
& 5.30pm-10.30pm

Marco Polo

33, Dean Street, **Newcastle**
0191 232 5533

Price £24

Established on Dean Street for over 20 years, Marco Polo has developed and grown along with Newcastle's ever-increasing interest in Italian food. A largely pizza-pasta menu offers all the expected variations on the themes. Exuberantly decorated, this warren of a restaurant just goes on and on. The atmosphere is friendly, with loads to see at every turn. Plastic vines and grapes have been taken to humorous excess. Mermaids, matelots and ladies of the night crowd the walls and jostle for position with all the paraphernalia of Marco Polo's nautical adventures. Great for a family or party meal.

Map ref: B2   Open: Mon-Fri 12.00 am-2.30pm
& 5.30pm-11.00pm;
Sat 12.00 am-11.30pm

Matchams

Theatre Royal, Market Street, **Newcastle**
0191 244 2513

Price £20

The scene: an elegant, classical building, a first floor room just off the Dress Circle of the Theatre Royal, overlooking the hurly burly of Market Street. The set: rich, royal blue and gold carpet with warm, pale yellow walls and drapes, blond wood chairs and crisp white table linen. The occcasional sparkle of silver cutlery and polished glasses greet the eye. The cast: friendly waiters calmly delivering an efficient service. The plot: top quality ingredients are cooked and translated into imaginative plate-design and brought to the table in dishes such as Goats cheese, roasted beetroot and lentil salad; Pan fried fillet of cod with new potatoes and spinach - soy and spring onion vinaigrette. Set menu, 3 courses £14.95 but you must book in advance. One of the features of Matchams is that you can enjoy your starter and main course and, by arrangement, have your dessert and coffee during the interval. It adds an extra pleasure to a seat in the stalls.

Open: Mon-Sat 5.30pm-10.00pm   Map ref: B2

Metzzo

Rear of 7, Osborne Road, **Jesmond**
0191 281 4441

Price £20

Middle Eastern dishes spice up a largely Italian menu. This happy mix is reflected in the decor, murals of Roman goddesses and grand hookahs in the bar area. The upstairs dining room overlooks the courtyard and parking space. The ceilings are decorated with swirls of muted colours and the occasional cherub. Rugs draped across oak beams, moderate music and gentle lighting enhanced by candles create a warm, easy ambience. The specials are worth working through, particularly the Tiger prawn kebab and the Aubergine tower starters. The Crepe di Metzzo was memorable for its generous filling and the Creme brulee is one of the crispiest cream desserts around. It's good food served without fuss, at your pace.

Open: Mon-sat 12.00pm-2.30pm   Map ref: B1
& 5.30pm-10.20pm

M o d i

36, Leazes Park Road, **Newcastle**
0191 261 8927

Price £31

Over the past two years since Chris (he of the bon mot) and his partner, Roberto (chef extraordinaire) opened Modi the plaudits have not ceased ... and with good reason. Modi is a very good restaurant. The cool, chic decor, the intelligence and flair of the dishes and the wit of the front of house presentation bring together the well-founded confidence of this partnership. The menus are understated, not needing the unnecessary flourishes of description - the food speaks for itself. Artichoke, squid and herb salad or Braised venison ravioli with sage and butter to start. Entrées like Sliced sirloin with rosemary and grilled vegetables and Noisettes of lamb with tarragon, vegetable rissole and persillade demonstrate the artistry at work. Roberto excels at desserts, ringing the seasonal changes with aplomb. The set menus (2 course lunch+ wine £8.99 & dinner £11.25) are very good value. This is a small restaurant with a big future.

Map ref: B2   *Open: Mon-Sat 12.00pm-2.00pm last orders; Tues-Sat 6.00pm 10.00pm last order.*

Newcastle Marriott Hotel Gosforth Park - The Park Restaurant

High Gosforth Park, **Newcastle**
0191236 4111

Price £32

Surrounded by mature parkland and with all the deep-piled comforts of a luxury hotel, the restaurant has an established reputation for excellent food. The burgundy and cream dining room is a sumptuous backdrop to the range of classic and contemporary dishes on offer. Mille feuille of smoked salmon with chive mascarpone cheese with prawn and tomato salsa sits comfortably next to the more traditional Smoked Scottish salmon with lemon and capers. Entrées like Roasted cod with aubergine and lobster brown beer sauce feature with favourites like Roast best end of lamb. The desserts are equally varied and delicious. An extensive wine cellar matches the menu and the service is friendly and very polished.

Map ref: B1   *Open: 7 days 7.00pm-10.00pm Sunday 12.30pm-2.00pm*

Old Orleans

Percy Street, Haymarket, **Newcastle**
0191 230 3344

Price £24

Hi y'all. Step this way for the Deep South, a pastiche of antique Orleans with an alligator to boot: you're just a sip away from your first mint julep. A Cajun-Mexican-Mississippi-Lousiana theme runs through the menu. Buckets of prawns, crunchy nachos with melted cheese to start. Chicken, fish, steaks blackened, spiced, peppered in various ways. Ribs barbecued Old Southern Style, jambalaya, fajitas with all sorts of fillings and big salads. Sampler dishes, meant to be shared, give you a taste of everything. If it's a Gone With The Wind theme night you are after, this is the place.

Open: Mon-Sat 11.00 am-11.00pm;   Map ref: B2
Sun 12.00pm-10.30 pm

One-Eyed Jack's

54-56, Pilgrim Street, **Newcastle**
0191 222 0130

Price £19

A lively Mexican cantina with hanging lanterns, cowboy pictures and a moose head glowering from the walls. The large hall lends itself to parties or a chatty lunch but beware, it is very, very noisy; I had to shout across the table to be heard. Live bands at the weekend add to the atmosphere. Tortillas, fajitas, nachos and ribs are all served with a dash (or more) of chilli. The servings are generous and you're advised to share with a friend. The starters are a meal in themselves. A mountain of nachos with melted cheese and jalapenos, followed by Pulled pork pig Santa Fe (crisp fried minced pork with mushrooms and chilli rolled in a tortilla) and you'll not want dessert. If you do, the Pecan pie has its own tear-jerking history.

Open: Tues-Sat 12.00pm-1.45pm;   Map ref: B2
Tues-Wed 5.30pm-10.15pm;
Thurs-Sat 5.30pm-10.30pm or later

Restaurant Victoria

Grand Hotel, Tynemouth
0191 293 6666

The Grand Hotel is situated overlooking Tynemouth Bay and Long Sands. This glorious setting is a fitting location for the Restaurant with its sparkling chandeliers and elegance of bygone years.

The best of classic cuisine and innovative cooking for today using fresh market produce.

Sunday lunches with traditional roasts, A la Carte with a cosmopolitan flavour and a daily changing Table D'hote menu served with mouthwatering sweets prepared in the kitchens, all of this accompanied with a good selection of wines from our cellars.

The Grand has a long established reputation and a warm welcome awaits you.

Open:
Mon-Fri 12pm-2pm & 6.30pm-10pm
Saturday 12pm-2pm & 6.30pm-10pm
Sunday 12pm-3pm

Pacific Bar Café

12-22, Northumberland Road, **Newcastle**
0191245 0440

Price £19

A stunning exterior of towering glass matched by an ultra-modern interior of electric blues, greens and marbled pillars and curved chrome. This is the place to see and be seen. A scenic lift whisks you from the ground floor bar (where the action is) through the Mezzanine to the 'rooftop' cafe. The menu ranges from breakfasts through to dinner with light lunches along the way. The global cuisine offers pizza and pasta, burgers and Tex-Mex, vegetarian, oriental cuisine along with seafood and steaks, plus a childrens' menu and loads of sweet treats and coffees. Cocktails are becoming a strong feature of this 'you-can-get-it-all-here' café bar. Definitely spoilt for choice but be prepared to queue at lunch time, it's very popular.

Open: Mon- Sat 11.00am-11.00 pm; Sun 12.00am-10.50pm

Map ref: B2

Pani's Café Bar

61, High Bridge, **Newcastle**
0191 232 4366

Price £17

Tucked away along High Bridge, Pani's offers authentic Italian food cooked and presented in an imaginative modern style. You can get a quick meal if you're on a tight schedule, or take your time if a leisurely lunch or dinner is what you want. The setting is surreal with cavernous sweeps that twist and turn from room to room. The burble of friends' conversation fills this busy, friendly restaurant. Everybody meets and eats there and enjoys it. The daytime menu concentrates on soups, salads and ciabatta sandwiches: in the evening more substantial meals are on offer, and what a range. The Minestrone is marvellous and the Ciabatta Milanese has to be tasted to be believed. Not a pizza in sight - this is the real thing!

Open: Mon-Sat 10.00am-10.00pm

Map ref:17

79

Paradiso

3, Market Lane, **Newcastle**
0191 221 1240

Price £26

The narrow street door belies the extensive rooms upstairs. Chic, stained-glass booths create interesting spaces in the open plan. Bar stools constructed from heavy engineering, splashes of light and pools of shade, this stylish restaurant has the culinary confidence to combine Indian spiced cod with couscous and roasted vegetables - and make it work. They import their own olive oil to make fresh pesto and offer a broad menu bringing Morocco ever closer to Italy. Thai dishes feature too, making this an eclectic mix. A full-time baker makes all the breads on the premises. Paradiso has all the pazzazz of a truly original restaurant.

Map ref: B2   Open: Mon-Thurs 11.00am 10.30pm; Fri-Sat 11.00am-10.45pm

Pinocchio

61, Westgate Road, **Newcastle**
0191 232 0708

Price £22

Standing at the foot of Westgate Road the restaurant is a wonderland. Images from the original Pinocchio story garland the walls and any child (or adult) will be intrigued to piece it all together as they enjoy their meal. Very popular with nearby office workers, the restaurant offers an all-week early-bird menu for lunchtime and home-time; any one of four starters plus a pizza or pasta dish from the a la carte menu. The Pinocchio theme runs through with Steak Geppetto, Vitello Stromboli and Salmone a la Monstro. Some more unusual combinations like Haddock in tomato, onion and parsley sauce and Scampi in cream and Pernod challenge the more adventurous among us.

*Map ref: B2   Open: Mon-Sat 12.00pm-2.30pm
& 6.00pm-11.00pm,
Sun 12.00pm-2.00pm
& 6.00pm-10.30pm*

Prego Café and Brasserie

Sunderland Museum and Winter Gardens, Burdon Road, **Sunderland**
0191 564 1777

Price £18

Prego has three of the best views in Sunderland. On one side the city park, complete with Victorian bandstand and ornamental pond; on the other a tropical garden waterfall. Set in the modern Winter Gardens, Prego is fast becoming a very popular focus for mid-city dining. The colour scheme of terracotta and cream, modern bent-wood chairs and walls of glass, so you can enjoy the views, all go to create a relaxed, bistro character. The menu is varied, offering light lunches which are mainly pizza-pasta dishes but the evening menu has an altogether broader aspect. Avocado salad or Salmon wrapped in smoked salmon lead on to Confit of duck leg with roasted orange and mint pesto and Halibut steak with garlic and olive oil and lemon reduction. Desserts like Peach fool and Pear and ginger cake with vanilla ice cream round off the meal. Sunday lunch (£5.95) is very good value.

Open: Mon-Sat 10.00am-4.30pm & 6.00pm-10.30pm; Sun 12.00pm-4.30pm

Map ref: C2

Prima Pizza Pasta

40-46, The Side, **Newcastle**
0191 233 1011

Price £22

A unique feature of this restaurant is the dining area, built into a colossal stone railway arch and designed to create the feel of a balconied piazza. Diners also experience the rumble of passing trains along with the disco beat of this party pizzeria. The cabaret of chefs flipping dough and dancing with the exuberant waiters to loud music, mean that in the evenings there is a permanent party going on, whether you want one or not. The food is unpretentious and the atmosphere friendly but not the first choice for a quiet, relaxed meal. The menu offers a standard Italian range with no surprises. It's fast food in a few minutes or fast food and take your time.

Open: Mon- Fri 12.00pm-2.00pm & 5.30pm- 11.00pm; Sat 12.00pm-12,00am; Sun 5.30pm-11.00pm

Map ref: B2

81

Puccini

29, Pudding Chare, **Newcastle**
0191 232 1961

Price £18

From the violin on the shutters to the fanned accordions on the staircase, the musical theme runs throughout Puccini. Happily though, no singing waiters. The terrace-look main dining area leads into an interior room and through to a secluded tented room, for a more private meal. Freshly made pasta, herbs and parmesan help to make this an attractive city option. The weekday lunch special (2 courses for £4.50) is good value. The dinner menu carries a range of pizza/pasta plus some more up-market dishes like Trotta Mandoriata (trout with butter, almonds and wine) and a number of vegetarian options. Good for a quick lunch to keep you going or for a more leisurely evening meal.

Open: Mon- Sat 12.00pm-2.30pm & 5.30pm-10.30pm; Sun 6.00pm-10.00pm

Map ref: B2

Quay 35

35, The Side, **Newcastle**
0191 232 3848

Price £24

Designed with taste, gently lit, Mackintosh chairs and tables, soothing music and relaxed bustle make this an attractive, chic bistro.The lunch menu has an interesting selection of cooked and cold dishes and sandwiches, enough to make you want to linger. The evening menu is equally inviting with starters like Caramelised stilton and red onion tart with balsamic reduction and mixed leaf salad followed by Roast duck with smoked bacon, fennel and potato mash and sour cherry sauce. Fascinating combinations in the specials confirm the confident flair of the chef and he keeps ringing the changes so you have to keep going back to see what he's up to.

Open: Mon- Fri 5.00pm-10.00pm; Sat 5.00pm-10.30pm; Thurs-Sat 12.00pm-2.30pm

Map ref:B2

Raj Tandoori

31, Pudding Chare, **Newcastle**
0191 232 1450

Price £17

A gentle, mannerly welcome as you step into the serene comfort of this very tasteful restaurant. Muted tones and gentle music, comfortable chairs and well-spaced tables encourage you to stay for a lingering meal. The cuisine is based on the idea that the perfect curry is made with plenty of patience. The use of artificial colourants to produce vibrant reds is rejected in preference for the natural effects of fresh spices. The dishes show the quiet confidence of an expert team who know their cuisine and their style. The 3 course lunch menu at £4.50 and the 4 course happy hour menu (Sun-Fri: 6.00 - 9.00 pm) at £6.50 are very good value. The full menu carries a broad range of traditional dishes. An oasis in the busy heart of the city.

Open: Mon- Sat 12.00pm-2.20pm & 6.00pm-12.00am; Sun 6.00pm-12.00am

Map ref: B2

Ristorante Roma

22, Collingwood Street, Newcastle
0191 232 0612

Price £22

Newcastle's first and longest established Italian restaurant, the Roma prides itself on serving the best in Italian cuisine. The slightly dated decor belies the sharp and passionate attitude that the owner/chef has for good quality ingredients translated into the best dishes. Everything is made to order so you may have to wait a while but it is well worth it. The speciality of the house is veal. Try the Scallopine a la Mode du Chef (veal with mushrooms and artichokes in a white wine and cream sauce) one of nine veal dishes on offer. I had my first ever Tournedos Rossini here in 1972 and I can still remember it.

Open: Mon- Sat 12.00pm-2.00pm & 7.00pm-11.00pm; Sun 7.00pm-11.00pm

Map ref: B2

Romano's

Customs House, Mill Dam, **South Shields**
0191 427 5400

Price £23

Romano's, a well-established restaurant in the Old Customs House Theatre complex on the quayside, handy for Shields ferry-crossing stop. The riverside is reflected in the decor but a sophisticated Italian theme dominates, using figurative paintings and discreet gold leaf. Theatre-goers can enjoy a discounted pre-show meal if they present their ticket and you may bump into a few celebs about to go to work. The menu is mainsteam Italian. Besides the usual pizza-pasta, chicken, steak and seafood, catches of fresh fish find their way onto the specials menu. Romano's has it's own label house wine which is also available at its three sister restaurants.

Map ref: C1
Open: Mon- Sat 11.00am-2.00pm & 6.00pm-10.30pm; Sun 11.00am-2.00pm & 6.00pm-10.00pm

Rossini   PAPIE CITY

Rear of Brentwood Avenue, **Jesmond**
0191 281 3812

Price £26

Tucked away in a back lane in Jesmond, first timers are intrigued to discover Rossini. The globe-lit courtyard leads into a tented, conservatory dining area. The Italian connection is underscored by crooning tenors in the background. This musical restaurant (sister to Puccini) has a sophisticated look for that special meal, but equally relaxed for a mid-week treat. Do book ahead if you want a weekend table - it's very popular. Fish dishes are the chef's particular interest and feature strongly in the menus. From Zuppe de pesce (fresh mixed fish with mussels cooked in stock, white wine, tomato and garlic) through entrees like Spiedini tre colore (a skewer of swordfish, tuna and salmon char-grilled with mixed salad) - it's fish heaven. The chef calls a halt at the chilled desserts which are so good they sell themselves.

Map ref:B1
Open: Mon- Sat 12.00pm-2.30pm & 6.00pm-11.00pm Sun 1.00pm-9.00pm

Royal Circle

16-18 Stowell Street, **Newcastle**
0191 261 2300

Price £23

The elegant, rich red and gold decor with equally plush deep carpets create a luxurious feel to the dining room. Szechuan-Cantonese cuisine, with seafood being the house speciality. Using authentic recipes from the regions they offer a range of banquet menus, spiralling in size as the party increases. The restaurant has a traditional image and serves the expected dishes with the confidence gained from its twelve years in the business. If you want a livelier evening there is a private dining room downstairs with a karaoke system - which seems to be increasingly popular along the length of Stowell Street.

Open: Mon- Sat 12.00pm-2.00pm & 6.00pm-11.15pm;
Sun 6.30pm-11.15pm

Map ref: B2

Sabatini

25, King Street, **Newcastle**
0191 261 4415

Price £25

Light, airy feel in one dining room and a classy, antique Italian decor in the other, Sabatini spans the range. The extensive menu offers the usual pizza-pasta, polli and pesce and four types of garlic bread. The nine chicken dishes, seven fish and twelve veal and beef entrées come with any combination of sauces. There is also a separate vegetarian menu. Sabatini appeals to everyone from the quiet couple to large parties. The atmosphere is relaxed-formal, the waiters are very attentive and offer a smoothly flowing service from the moment you enter. The lunch-time set menu (2 courses plus coffee at £8.45) is an attractive proposition. A stylish affair from beginning to end.

Open: Mon- Thurs 5.30pm-10.30pm;
Fri-Sat 5.30pm-11.00pm

Map ref: B2

Sachins

Forth Banks, Newcastle
0191 261 9035

Price £23

Good Punjabi cuisine is alive and well at Sachins. Set behind Central Station and on the rise from the river, it specialises in slow-cooked dishes infused with delicate blends of Indian spices. The menu looks like many others but the difference lies in the detail, so book a table because the regulars fill the place night after night. Set meals guide you through the range of dishes on offer and give you a chance to sample several. Be adventurous and branch out. Try one of the chef's specialities like Chooza lucknawi (a full baby chicken cooked in lucknawi spices, stuffed with minced chicken and served with a mild sauce), it sounds so exotic, or one of the tandoori dishes, which are renowned for their fragrance. The nans are spectacular and a must with whatever you choose.

Map ref: B2

Open: Mon- Sat 12.00pm-2.15pm & 6.00pm-11.15pm

Sale Pepe

115, St George's Terrace, Jesmond
0191 281 1431

Price £19

Tomato rich walls, splashes of Michaelangelo across the ceiling and large, fruit-encrusted mirrors add a dash of Mediterranean artistry to this Jesmond restaurant. The busy main dining area has an offshoot for those who want a quieter time. The test of Sale Pepe is its loyal following: customers just keep on coming back for more. Maybe that's a reflection on the menu which offers a broad range of very reasonably priced meals. There are no big surprises but the servings are generous and the quality good. Starters like Gamberoni con aglio (king prawns in garlic, white wine and parsley served with rice) are matched with entrees like Spaghetti con gorgonzola, which rings the changes by introducing walnuts into the spinach and cream sauce. Parking nearby is easy - always a bonus.

Map ref: B1

Open: Mon-Sat 11.00am-11.00pm; Sun 12.00pm-10.30pm

Shiremoor House Farm

Middle Engine Lane, **New York**
0191 257 6302

Price £23

For many years the Shiremoor House Farm has had a well-deserved reputation for serving good food. The extensively modernised Victorian farmhouse retains much of the character of the original building. The food is consistently good and the menus offer a wide and varied range of dishes from the traditional Steak, ale and mushroom casserole to the more exotic Mexican style lamb with rice. The vegetarian menu is just as imaginative with Sizzling quorn in a sweet and sour sauce or Vegetarian sausages on champ with a rich onion gravy. They carry guest ales, supplied by the nearby, award-winning Mordue Brewery. There is a company policy of no background music so families, friends and those wanting a quiet meal can enjoy the sound of their own conversations.

Open: Mon-Sat 11.00am-11.00pm;   Map ref: C1
Sun 12.00 pm-10.30pm

The Side Café Bistro

1-3, The Side, **Newcastle**
0191 261 4224

Price £21

Bistro-style cosmopolitan dishes with the unique feature of a cinema at the back of the restaurant. The only place in town where you can combine Cajun chicken with celluloid greats. Downstairs you can sit in the window and watch the world go by and there's another dining room upstairs where arched windows overlook the action. The menu has starters like Salmon fish cakes with caper salad and French vinaigrette. The entrées invite a close-up: Lamb cutlets on a bed of buttered mash, mushrooms and bab gounash and the desserts are starlets in their own right. There are plans to have themed nights when Cocteau will be accompanied with coq au vin. The cinema even has smoochy double seats in the back row. I'm ready Mr De Mille!

Open: Mon 11.00am-3.00pm;   Map ref:B2
Tues-Sat 11.00am-3.00pm &
5.30pm-10.00pm

Sidney's Restaurant

3, Percy Park Road, **Tynemouth**
0191 257 8500

Price £28

Sidney's is one of Tynemouth's surprisingly small number of good restaurants. The striking purple exterior is carried through into the bold interior design. Clean lines in the table settings, stylish furniture and warm natural tones create a super-bistro feel to the place. The menu has a great range of imaginative dishes all freshly cooked to order: Honey roast duck with noodle, baby corn and plum salad to start followed by Monkfish saltimbocca, garlic roast new potatoes and salsa verdi. Desserts like Chocolate-stuffed prune tart and vanilla ice cream entice you on. Lunchtime menus offer special price ranges from two courses £6.95 to three courses for £10.95 and there's even more choices on the blackboard specials. There is a key on the menu suggesting which wine complements each dish: at this award-winning restaurant they think of everything.

Map ref: C1

Open: Mon-Fri 12.00pm-2.30pm & 6.00pm-10.00pm; Sat 12.00pm-3.00pm & 6.00pm-10.00pm

Simla Tandoori

39, The Side, **Newcastle**
0191 232 1070

Price £26

Traditional Indian cuisine in a traditional Indian setting. The distinctive feature about Simla is that it has an extended licence and stays open into the wee small hours. Long-established (18 years) on the Quayside circuit of restaurants, it is ideally situated to feed those night-clubbers who need refuelling after a heavy session on the dance floor. Simla also has a regular band of customers happy to return again and again. Take the worry out of choosing with a banquet menu for two or four offering a good range of popular starters and main dishes.

Map ref: B2

Open: Mon-Thurs 6.00pm-2.30am; Fri-Sat 6.00pm-3.00am; Sun 7.00pm-12.30am

Sitar

Whites Hotel, 38-42, Osborne Road, **Jesmond**
0191 281 0458

Price £21

Osborne Road is the "in" place. Most nights the strip is buzzing with good natured crowds moving from bar to bar or enjoying one of the many restaurants in the area. Sitar is at the heart of this night life and yet is a quiet pocket within the hurly burly. Tasteful, muted jewel colours of reds and golds with crucibles of fluttering flame light are the backdrop to your meal. The dishes are recognisable to the seasoned diner but the surprise lies in the quality and delicacy of the flavouring. The robust oranges and reds of the sauces belie the fragrant subtlety of the chef's light touch. The Chicken Sitar special is a good example of this, as is the King prawn balti, both trumpeting their importance with flamboyant flourish but, in reality, being delicate blends of crushed spices and shredded herbs that enliven the meat and shellfish. By the way, Sitar makes the biggest, puffiest Peshwari Nans - to my mind the benchmark of a good Indian restaurant.

*Open: 7 days 12.00pm-2.00pm
6.00pm-12.00am*

Map ref: B2

Spice A La Carte

Scottish Life House, 11, Archbold Terrace, **Jesmond**
0191 281 9988

Price £24

The image is modern and vibrant, the decor a daring fusion of bright Indian jewel colours in a contemporary western style. The walls carry blocks of acid green, warm orange and rich purple all subtly lit to create an overall effect that this is a relaxed, confident place to be. That confidence is reflected in the cuisine which has an innovative approach to popular Indian cooking. As well as the old favourites we all know and love, there are newcomers like Shahi Machli (prawns touched with home-made chutney, wrapped in smoked salmon, served with creamy marsalla sauce) where the chef struts his stuff. Everything is done with style. Santana not sitars in the background: the sign of things to come.

*Open: 7 days 12.00pm-3.00pm;
Mon-Sat 5.50pm-11.30pm;
Sun 6.00pm-11.30pm.*

Map ref:B1

Tantalus

7, Higham Place, **Newcastle**
0191 232 4949

Price £2

The motto of Tantalus is that they serve "food the gods won't punish you for" because it's all low calorie and healthy, from the lunchtime sandwiches (eat in or take away) through to the Fillet of beef Wellington, everything has the Tantalus seal of approval. The decor is crisp and clean, with original modern art adding swirling splashes of colour to the neutral walls. Wedgwood blue sofas, tiles and gauzy drapes add accent and highlight. The recipes ring the changes with Poached asparagus served with honey and mustard dressing or Seared king scallops with tantalising lime and peppercorn coulis to start. Trout and almond crumble or Vegetarian traunch (quorn, spinach and nutmeg served with a tomato salsa) follow. Desserts like Passion fruit and mango choux pastry may tempt you from the straight and narrow, but we all need to fall sometimes, and what a good way to go!

Map ref: B2   Open: Mon-Sat 11.00am-2.30pm
Thurs-Sat 6.00pm-10.00pm

Thai Siam

14, Stowell Street, **Newcastle**
0191 232 0261

Price £2

The discreet art of welcome is at the door with bowing statues. Building on the holiday experiences of the well travelled North-Eastener, Thai Siam brings a pleasant variation to the oriental theme of Stowell Street. Spicier than Cantonese food and not as hot as Indian, Thai cuisine is a pleasant blend of the best of both. Authentic recipes served by waitresses in traditional costume. Everything from the sequinned elephants to the Steamed salmon with steak with herbs and chilli and Roast duck with soy sauce, vegetables and pickled sweet ginger are waiting to be discovered. The banquet menus are probably the best way to sample the dishes - the larger the party the larger the choice - and it's all a little bit different.

Map ref: B2   Open: Mon-Sat 12.00pm-2.15pm
& 6.30pm-11.15pm
Sun 6.30pm-10.30pm

Throwing Stones

National Glass Centre, Dame Dorothy Street, **Sunderland**
0191 565 3939

rice £21

This ironically named restaurant is part of the ultra-modern National Glass Centre on the banks of the river Wear, so you can combine a look at the striking glass sculptures and glassblowers at work with a good meal. The menu offers everything from light lunches of rolled tortilla and open sandwiches to a full a la carte dinner. Concentrating on the latter, you can enjoy dishes like Galia melon with feta cheese and raspberries, served with a chive balsamic dressing followed by Mussels in a white wine, cream and coriander sauce, served with cheesy French bread toasts. Unusual combinations demonstrate the chef's confident style. Desserts are just as imaginative with Hazelnut iced soufflé with vanilla sauce and tuille biscuit and Dark chocolate cheesecake with candied fruit and a burnt orange sauce. Doesn't that sound good?

Open: 7 days 10.00am-5.00pm;
ri & Sat 7.00pm-11.00pm

Map ref: C2

Treacle Moon

5-7, The Side, **Newcastle**
0191 232 5537

rice £38

Treacle Moon is named after Byron's description of his honeymoon at Seaham Hall, an experience too sweet to be merely honey. The dining room with slate-lavender walls, crisp white linen and silver tableware is calm and very stylish without being overly self-concious. Starters include such treats as Tempura and sesame seed king prawns with spicy mango coulis. The luxury goes on with entrées such as Rosemary oil grilled turbot, saffron crushed potato, garlic comfit and red pepper puree. Why not round off the experience with Dark chocolate fondant with white chocolate sorbet? You know you want to.

Open: Mon-Fri 6.00pm-1.00am;
at 5.30pm-1.00am

Map ref: B2

Treasure of the Orient

26-28 Stowell Street, **Newcastle**
0191 230 4008

Price £2

A giant statue of a happy Buddha greets you at the door. There are hints of Chinese heritage in the glass screens and golden dragon-shields on the walls. The interior is a happy mix of ancient and modern styles - chic Chinoise. The chef is grounded in Cantonese and Pekinese cuisine and has also worked in Paris. He brings a blend of his experience to the menu, his special dish being Aromatic crispy duck. There is a range of banquet menus, including a special for £9.50 per person, all served with Ham fried rice and followed by Jasmine tea. Quiet twosomes, family groups and parties with karaoke are catered for but you are advised to book ahead.

Map ref:B2

Open: Mon-Fri 12.00pm-2.00pm & 6.00pm-11.00pm; Sat 12.00pm 11.00pm; Sun 12.00pm-10.30pm

Uno's

18, Sandhill, **Newcastle**
0191 261 5264

Price £1

Set right at the heart of Newcastle's Quayside club-life, Uno's is always busy. Situated just below street level, a series of rooms twist and turn in a fascinating warren. Celebrity graffiti on the walls (plus the occasional celebrity in person) and an eclectic mix of pictures, photographs and statues, some life-size, create an effect of relaxed jumble, a lived-in feel. The menu carries the usual pizza-pasta range with 12 slightly more upmarket chicken, prawn and steak dishes, plus all the old favourites for dessert. Happy hour and Sunday lunch bargains. Servings are generous, prices are very reasonable and the staff are friendly and attentive which explains why it is so popular.

Map ref: B2

Open: Mon- Sat 12.00pm 11.00pm; Sun 12.00pm-2.00pm 6.00pm-10.30pm

Valley Junction 397

Archbold Terrace, **Jesmond**
0191 281 6397

rice £25

Sharing the railway theme with its sister restaurant in Corbridge, Valley Junction is uniquely situated in an Edwardian railway carriage and signal box in what was once Jesmond Station. Chic, relaxed, sumptuous interior plus a very polished service have made this an extremely successful restaurant. The menu offers an excellent range of dishes, some the chef's own recipes, like Luari Mangsho (a medium hot lamb dish cooked with tomato, peppers and fresh coriander) and Duck Masallam (duck breast marinated in herbs, cooked and served in a creamy coconut sauce). Be sure to book, with only 15 tables seating is limited.

pen: Tues- Sat 12.00pm-2.00pm   Map ref: B1
6.00pm-11.30pm;
un 6.00pm-11.30pm

Vermont Hotel - Blue Room

Castle Garth, **Newcastle**
0191 233 1010

rice £42

Everything you would expect from a restaurant that has received countless accolades from all the major food guides. The sophisticated dining room is richly decorated in deep blue and gold. A formal setting with a relaxed atmosphere, the menu blends classic French with contemporary international cuisine. Roasted scallops with ginger and coriander risotto, Truffle tart with poached quail eggs and panchetta salad to start. Northumbrian canon of lamb, artichoke barigoule, truffle gnocchi, garlic and rosemary jus. It's poetry! The desserts wax lyrical and so will you when you taste the Kirsch iced parfait with compote of marinated black cherries or the Raspberry creme brulée with basil Anglaise. The menu is changed seasonally. This highly-rated restaurant is justifiably confident of its place.

pen: Tues-Sat 6.30pm-10.00pm   Map ref: B2
st orders

Vujon

29, Queen Street, **Newcastle**
0191 2210601

Price £3

Set in the heart of the trendy Quayside, the luxurious sofas and richly draped windows establish the quality of Vujon the moment you enter. The ground floor dining room is sophisticated and elegant. Downstairs there is a self-contained, opulent dining room with its own bar for private parties. Highly professional waiters offer an excellent service to the discerning diner. Vujon means "gourmet dinner" and the restaurant is aptly named. The main menu reflects a range of dishes from every Indian region with some unusual combinations. Sas ni macchi (tuna kebab with herbs and spices, garnished with onion and peppers) to start, followed by a rich treat of Pasanda Mughali (lamb cooked in fresh cream, cultured yoghurt and almonds). The menu offers everything from a finger buffet to a reasonably priced set menu through to the vast range of the a la carte.

Map ref: B2

Open: Mon- Sat 12.00pm
2.30pm; & 6.00pm-11.30pm
Sun 7.00pm-11.00pm

Waterside Palace

29, Forth Banks, **Newcastle**
0191 232 6090

Price £3

A fantasy pagoda, the Waterside Palace is resplendent in red and green. Purpose built in 1996, it's everyone's idea of what a Chinese restaurant should be. The striking colours are reflected in more muted tones inside where occasional carved screens and lanterns fringe the dining room which overlooks the Tyne. A wonderful array of banquet menus to suit every palate and purse, plus an impressive a la carte menu. Where this restaurant differs is in its range of meat and seafood dishes. Roast duck with plum sauce, Lamb in satay sauce with hot pot, Blue shell crab with black bean sauce, Fresh whole seabass steamed with ginger and spring onion in soya sauce. Sounds so poetic. Chopsticks are the order of the day, knife and fork optional.

Map ref: B2

Open: 7 days 12.00pm-11.00pm

*BOARDWALK CAFE
Little Haven Hotel, River Drive, South Shields
Tel: (0191) 455 4455 www.littlehavenhotel.com
Open daily 7am-6pm
The cafe is located within a conservatory within the hotel overlooking the sea and so offers some lovely views. The cafe serves traditional English breakfasts and a range of home-made sandwiches, snacks and desserts - the cheesecake comes highly recommended. An a la carte menu is also served in the evening.
Map ref: C1

CHARLOTTE'S TEA ROOMS
172 Park View, Whitley Bay
Tel: (0191) 280 2607
Open daily 9.30am-4pm. This cosy tea room has a real fire and serves a good selection of home-made food - ideal to warm up after a chilly afternoon walk by the coast.
Map ref: C1

*GIBSIDE TEA ROOM
Near Burnopfield, Newcastle
Tel: (01207) 542255 www.nationaltrust.org.uk
Open 10am-5pm Tuesday to Sunday (open Bank Holiday Mondays)
This tea room is located at the 18th century Gibside estate, originally inhabited by the Bowes Lyon family. It's ideal before or after a walk around the estate gardens or the woodland river walk. The tea room, which serves a small range of light snacks is also attached to a National Trust Gift shop and sometimes displays work from local artists.
Map ref: A2

*JARROW HALL CAFE
Bede's World, Church Bank, Jarrow
Tel: (0191) 489 2106 www.bedesworld.co.uk
Open 10am-4pm (and from 12pm on Sunday)
Jarrow Hall, an 18th century house, is located within Bede's World which tells the extraordinary life of the Venerable Bede who lived there 1,300 years ago. The Hall houses a café serving light snacks and sandwiches and offers an ideal resting point while exploring the site. Photos in the hall also depict the family who used to live there.
Map ref: C2

OODLES
22a Front St, Tynemouth
Tel: (0191) 257 0090
Open 10am-5pm daily
This small tea room is well situated for a stroll along Tynemouth beach and is also attached to a small deli. Combine your visit with a look around Tynemouth's gift shops, neighbouring Priory and market within the Metro station.
Map ref: C1

*SOUTER LIGHTHOUSE TEA ROOM
Coast Road, Whitburn
Tel: (0191) 529 3161 www.nationaltrust.org.uk
Open 11am-5pm (excluding Fridays)
Climb the 76 steps of the 19th century Souter

Lighthouse and you can look out to the sea for miles around. Afterwards get your feet back on the ground with a walk along the coastal paths and a light snack at this tea room which serves light lunches, home-made cakes and local delicacies such as 'singin hinnies'.
Map ref: C2

RAFTERS COFFEE SHOP
Land of Green Ginger, Tynemouth
Tel: (0191) 257 2051
Open 10am-4pm daily
This coffee shop is housed within a 19th century church on Front Street in Tynemouth. Contained within the church are shops selling books, antiques, bric-a-brac and gifts. The tea room is on the first floor so there is no wheelchair access.
Map ref: C1

RAINTON MEADOWS COFFEE SHOP
Rainton Meadows Nature Reserve, Chilton Moor Houghton-le-Spring
Tel: (0191) 584 3112
Open 11am-4pm daily
Rainton Meadows used to be an open-cast coal site until 1985 when it closed down. It has now been transformed into a nature reserve and visitor centre with a tea room which serves light snacks. It's an ideal resting point following a walk around the reserve
Map ref: C3

THE TEA ROOMS
4 Marden Road, Whitley Bay
Tel: (0191) 252 3943
Open 10am-4pm daily
This traditional tea room is located opposite St Paul's church within five minutes walk to the beach and the local attractions of Whitley Bay. They serve a good selection of pastries, cakes and light meals.
Map ref: C1

VICTORIAN TEA ROOMS
Chandlers Garden Centre,
High Gosforth Park
Tel: (0191) 217 0786
Open 10am-4pm Mon to Sat 10.30am-4pm Sun
Located within the garden centre, this traditional tea room offers cream teas and flavoured scones with real fresh cream. Hand crafted gifts are also on sale within the tea room.
Map ref: B1

*WATERSIDE CAFE
Wild Fowl and Wetlands Trust,
District 15 Washington
Tel: 0191 416 5454 www.wwt.org.uk/washington
Open 10am-4pm daily
This tea room offers beautiful, panoramic views of the colourful wildfowl and serves full lunches, light snacks and coffees/teas. Sunday lunches are also on the menu.
Map ref: B2

Northumbria Tourist Board member

Places to eat in Durham

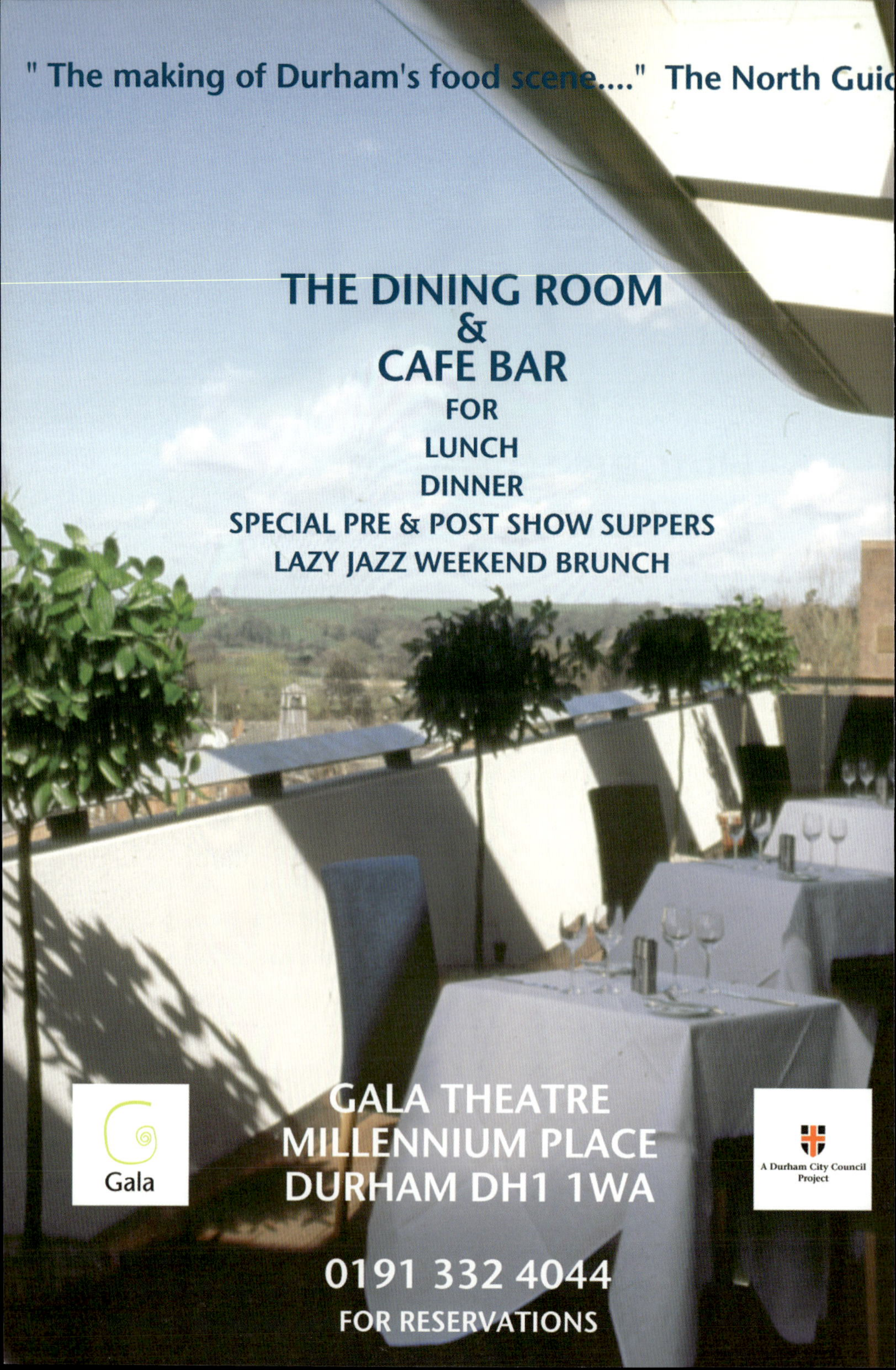

" The making of Durham's food scene...." The North Guid
THE DINING ROOM
&
CAFE BAR
FOR
LUNCH
DINNER
SPECIAL PRE & POST SHOW SUPPERS
LAZY JAZZ WEEKEND BRUNCH
Gala
GALA THEATRE
MILLENNIUM PLACE
DURHAM DH1 1WA
A Durham City Council Project
0191 332 4044
FOR RESERVATIONS

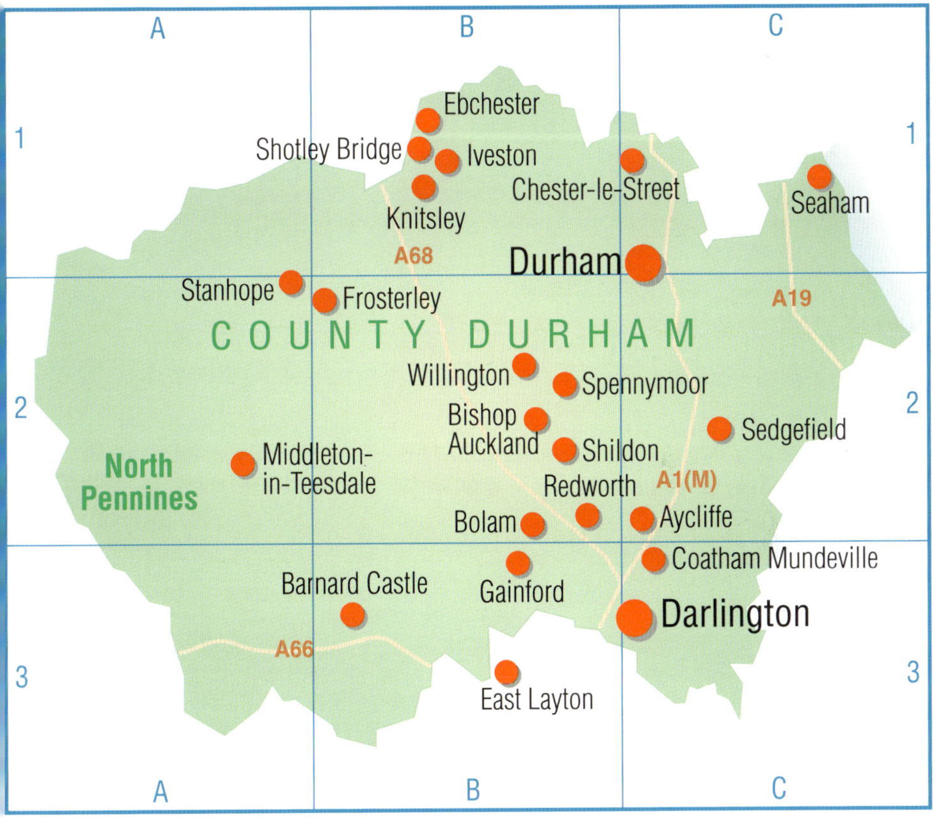
A
B
C
1
1
2
2
3
3
Ebchester
Shotley Bridge
Iveston
Chester-le-Street
Seaham
Knitsley
A68
Durham
Stanhope
Frosterley
A19
COUNTY DURHAM
Willington
Spennymoor
Bishop
Auckland
Sedgefield
Shildon
North
Pennines
Middleton-
in-Teesdale
Redworth
A1(M)
Bolam
Aycliffe
Coatham Mundeville
Barnard Castle
Gainford
Darlington
A66
East Layton
A
B
C

MINISTERS RESTAURANT

MARK AND **MANDY** WOULD LIKE
TO WELCOME YOU TO
MINISTERS RESTAURANT.

SITUATED IN THE CENTRE OF SEDGEFIELD, IT'S THE
PLACE TO DINE. WHETHER IT IS FOR A LIGHT LUNCH, OR
A SPECIAL DINNER, MINISTERS HAS SOMETHING FOR
EVERYONE.

LUNCH IS SERVED FROM
12 PM UNTIL 2 PM TUESDAY TO FRIDAY,
CHOOSING EITHER ONE, TWO, OR THREE COURSE
LUNCHES WITH
COFFEE, FROM £8.00 PER PERSON

DINNER IS SERVED FROM
7 PM UNTIL 9.30 PM TUESDAY TO SATURDAY
A FULL Á LA CARTE MENU AND A FIVE-COURSE TABLE
D'HÓTE MENU (£24.50) ARE AVAILABLE.

ON SUNDAY WE SERVE A TRADITIONAL FOUR-COURSE
SUNDAY LUNCH FROM 12 PM UNTIL 2 PM.
£12.95 FOR ADULTS, £6.95 FOR CHILDREN.

Ministers Restaurant,
8 Church View, Sedgefield, Co. Durham, TS21 2AY
Tel:- (01740) 622201

Almshouses

Palace Green, **Durham**
0191 3861054

Price £9.50 (three course lunch)

Open all year, seven days a week, providing morning coffee, lunch and afternoon teas. In the summer months the opening hours extend into the evening with an early supper menu similar to the lunchtime dishes. Try a Sunday morning stroll across the green to the magnificent Durham Cathedral and saunter into the cafe for a relaxed breakfast and a read of the café's newspapers. Stay for lunch and have Sweet potato, apple and ginger soup, or Hot pork and leek sausage sandwich - or both if you're really hungry. The desserts, like all the dishes, are freshly made and delicious. The Brazil nut pavlova is worth a try but you may have to walk a few times round the cathedral to burn off those calories.

Open: 7 days 9.00am-5.00pm; Easter- Sept 9.00am-8.00pm

Map ref: C1

Bistro 21

Aykley Heads House, **Aykley Heads**
0191 384 4354

Price £30

This is the place for food of the highest quality. The sand-gold building, imaginatively converted from an old country villa, is tucked away on the edge of Durham City, but is well known, being part of Terry Laybourne's 21 chain, and shares its reputation for excellence. Ten starters (£4.50 - £8.50) include a spinach and cheddar soufflé to die for. From the main courses (£11.50 - £14.50) try the refreshing Char-grilled breast of chicken with spiced couscous, yoghurt and mint or the Teriyaki-grilled salmon with noodles and fresh herb tempura. Some unusual farmhouse cheeses, homemade ice creams, or one of the other ten desserts (£3.50 - £5.00) - each dish is a winner. Coffee in the enclosed courtyard - a little Provencal pocket.

Open: Mon-Fri 7.00pm-10.30pm; Sat 6.00pm-10.30pm

Map ref: C1

Casa Nostra

36, Cockton Hill Road, **Bishop Auckland**
01388 609292

Price £20

The colourful Vince Barbaro owns and cooks in his equally colourful restaurant, where diners are surrounded by murals of luscious fruits and Mediterranean scenes. Locals call this Mr B's - for obvious reasons. He prepares a wide range of pizza-pasta dishes with a few special twists. For example, Arancio, a pasta sauce which is a mix of orange, almonds, spring onions, mushrooms, chicken, aniseed and cream cheese, and a chicken dish, Inferno, presumably because the chilli pepperoni is as hot as Hades. Mr B. is also prepared to cook any combination of ingredients to order.

Map ref: B2   *Open: 7 days 5.30pm-12.00 am*

The Countryman Inn

Bolam, Nr. Darlington
01388 834577

Price £2

The tiny village of Bolam is the setting for this inn-based restaurant. Chef, David Clarke and his partner, Mary Bowles, have developed a cosmopolitan menu and have an enthusiastic following. David's passion for trying new dishes shows in the menu with Pan seared scallop and smoked bacon salad with parmesan croutons and balsamic vinaigrette - not exactly run-of-the-mill pub food. Entrées like Oven roast pork fillet with spiced caramelised apples, honey mustard and calvados reduction support the point, as does the Pan fried duck breast with red onion marmalade, Toulouse sausage and red wine sauce. Servings are generous. Desserts are just as varied with tarts, custards, home-made ice cream and good unpasteurised British cheeses. To top it all, they also hold several awards for their real ales! The perfect focus for a run out in the countryside.

Map ref: B2   *Open: Summer - Tues-Sun*
12.00pm-2.00pm & 7.00pm-9.30
last orders
Winter-Sat-Sun 12.00pm-2.00pm &
Tues-Sat 7.00pm-9.30 last orders

The County

13, The Green, **Aycliffe Village**
01325 312273

Price £28

Chef/patron Andrew Brown is justly proud of The County's award-winning restaurant; it really is a world away from traditional pub food. The reason why is revealed when you read the menu. Not many pubs serve starters like Wensleydale blue, sweet pear and walnut salad or Freshwater crayfish tails bound in tarragon and lemon mayonnaise dressed leaves. Entrées go on to confirm this view, with Chargrilled loin of tuna served with spiced couscous and basil dressing or Roast chump of lamb with a herb crust, chargrilled vegetables, gremolata mash and rosemary gravy. As if more proof were needed, the luxury desserts push home the point. The bar menu offers a similarly interesting range of dishes, which makes this a cut above the rest and definitely worth a visit.

Open: 7 days 12.00pm-2.00pm
& 6.00pm-9.30pm

Map ref: C2

Durham Marriott Hotel Royal County - Royal County Restaurant & Cruz Brasserie

Old Elvet, **Durham City**
0191 386 6821

Price £31 Royal County - £21 Cruz Brasserie

The hotel offers a choice of dining: traditional, haute cuisine and informal, relaxed bistro-style. The Royal County restaurant has all the luxury of silver service with a grand piano rippling away in the background. Diners here enjoy neo-classic dishes like Salad of smoked salmon with caper shallot and parsley dressing followed by Fillet of lamb with roast Mediterranean vegetables and gnocchi potatoes, plus all the 'surf and turf' favourites. The Cruz brasserie has a lighter, contemporary feel with a menu to match. Garlic and artichoke ciabatta crostini and Sweet pepper and roast tomato soup with creme fraiche set the tone. Entrées like Clam and prawn paella and Baked chicken with garganelli pasta, tomatoes, olives and parmesan carry it through to dessert and coffee. Booking is advisable at weekends but you can always chance turning up and seeing which one you fancy.

Open: Royal County 7 days
12.30pm-2.15pm & 7.15pm-10.15pm
Cruz Brasserie Mon - Fri 12.00 pm-
9.30 pm; Sat-Sun 12.30 pm-9.30 pm

Map ref:1

Hall Garth Golf & Country Club Hotel - Hugo's Restaurant

Coatham Mundeville, Darlington
01325 300400

Price £3?

The Summerson's family home has been transformed into a luxury country house hotel and award-winning restaurant, set in extensive grounds with a 9-hole, parkland golf course. Got the picture - it's spacious and super-comfy. The interior is more of the same with log fires in winter and sumptuous sofas for relaxing, pre-dinner drinks. The menu continues the theme with some interesting dishes, and descriptions, on offer. Start with Fresh Whitby crab and avocado married with a light vinaigrette spiked with star burst bubbles of pink grapefruit or perhaps the Warm salad of calves liver with sautéed day-glo pink stalks of tender rhubarb deglazed with Grenadine syrup. Simpler sounding entrées, like Pan fried pork with creamed morels and wild rice pilau and the desserts just roll off (or onto) the tongue. Try the delicious Warm apricot clatoutis with vanilla ice cream or Oven roasted butterscotch bananas "en papilote" with creme fraiche. A luxurious experience.

Map ref: C3   *Open: 7 days 7.00pm-10.00pm*
Sun 12.00pm-2.00pm

Headlam Hall

Nr. **Gainford**, Darlington
01325 730238

Price £3?

This 17th century, Jacobean mansion is set in four acres of walled garden and surrounded by rolling farmland. The nearby hamlet of Headlam completes the rural idyll. The restaurant spreads through a series of different rooms, offering everything from a party venue to intimate dining. The impressive menu ranges through English and continental cuisine, plus daily specials, using local produce wherever possible. A Strudel of spinach, red onion and mozzarella cheese served with a tomato salsa to start or some Loch Fyne smoked salmon with lemon mayonnaise. A delicate Citrus sorbet or demi-tasse of soup to clear the palate and on to Roast breast of pheasant on a plum and celeriac rosti with a bacon and shallot sauce or maybe the Chef's beef dish of the day. Save room for a dessert; Vanilla bavarois with poached soft fruit or an indulgent Sticky toffee pudding with dark pecan sauce and home-made vanilla ice cream. Everything is presented with great style and well-placed confidence.

Map ref: B3   *Open: 7 days 7.00pm-9.3?*

Kings Head Bistro

52-53 Market Place, **Middleton-in-Teesdale**
01833 640467

Price £18

Middleton is a delightful village in an area of oustanding natural beauty, referred to as the "gateway to the Pennines". Wonderful walking country and with plenty of places of interest nearby (Bowes Museum and High Force waterfall) there is always something to see and do. The Kings Head is at the top of that list when it comes to eating out. The menu offers an interesting mix of traditional recipes with imaginative contemporary twists. For example, Game terrine with venison, orange coulis and English chutney caviar or Wild mushroom soup served with croutons to start. Entrées like Pork loin forestiere with sherry, cream and mushroom infused with tarragon or old favourites like Half shoulder of lamb in a rich minted gravy, all served with fresh, seasonal vegetables. To finish off, desserts like Apricot tartlet or Passion fruit bavarois, served with cream. The pricing policy states that they charge enough to ensure they survive but little enough to make sure you come back, again and again. Why not put it to the test?

Open: 7 days 12.00pm-2.00pm & 6.00pm-11.00pm

Map ref: A2

Knights Restaurant

Kingslodge Hotel, Waddington Street, Flass Vale, **Durham City**
0191 370 9999

Price £35

From the rich yellow exterior to the muted Monet shades of the dining room this restaurant exudes sophistication. Glass sculptures and discreet lighting create a contemporary, relaxed feel to this very chic restaurant - all of which qualities are reflected in the inventive menu. Starters include Tempura of king prawns with a trio of complementary home-made sauces and Fresh Loch Fyne oysters with a selection of accompaniments. Fish, meat and poultry main courses such as Lobster with beurre noisette and lemon and Saddle of venison with roasted figs and chestnuts are a couple of examples of what is on offer. The desserts continue the innovative character of this restaurant with Parfait of apple and peppermint with roasted strawberries and Praline cheesecake. The menu may be 'haute' but the atmosphere is anything but stuffy and the live music often encourages diners to dance. At £19.95 the Table D'hote is good value.

Open: Mon - Sat 6.30 pm-10.30 pm & Sun 7.00pm- 9.30pm.

Map ref: C1

Durham

La Famiglia

77 Parkgate, **Darlington**
01325 467991

Price £25

This family-run restaurant is situated close to the theatre and arts centre of the town and organises its opening hours to match the needs of the theatre-going public. It offers pre- and after-show menus which carry a wide range of traditional Sicilian dishes plus the usual pizza options. Seafood starters like Deep fried calamari bring back memories of summer holidays and the Pollo Siciliano (breast of chicken in aubergine, peppers, chilli, tomato and white wine sauce) is like mamma used to make - and still does here. The atmosphere is relaxed and very informal: a good choice for a classic cannelloni or a friendly farfalle. The early evening menu (Mon-Fri ; £7.25) is a bargain.

Map ref: C3   Open: Mon - Sat 5.30pm-10.30pm

Lumley Castle - Black Knight Restaurant

Chester-le-Street
0191 389 1111

Price £37

It doesn't get more imposing than this - a medieval castle in rolling parkland. The deep rose coloured decor of the luxurious lounges, the elegant, candlelit dining room overlooking the lordly demesne; every detail is authentic with a menu to match. The dishes are equally grand: starters like Wild mushroom soufflé with a tomato and basil coulis. Entrées such as Tournados of beef Lumley, fillet with stilton wrapped in bacon on a dauphinoise of potato in a port wine sauce or Grilled lemon sole with sweet pepper and lemon butter. Desserts are all freshly made and there is a rich cheeseboard selection. The medieval backdrop makes the whole experience much more than just dining out.

*Map ref: C1   Open: Sun- Fri 12.00pm-1.45pm
last orders
7 days 7.00pm-9.45pm*

Ministers Restaurant

8, Church View, **Sedgefield**
01740 622201

Price £32

Alluding to the area's M.P. Tony Blair or to its proximity to the village church - take your pick, either way, Ministers is a cut above the rest. The interior is a blend of restful rich reds with classy cream and touches of gold. The English/French menu has a wealth of dishes. Game soup flavoured with herbs and port, baked with a pastry crust just as a starter! Main course dishes read like chapter and verse of the culinary bible. Verse 1: Lattice of lemon sole and salmon lightly steamed with tarragon with a saffron and champagne sabyon and aniseed scented mussels. Verse 2: Tenderloin of wild boar roasted with orange zest, with caramelised apple and a roast game sausage. They taste even better than they sound ... and it doesn't stop there because the desserts are just as tempting. To paraphrase Harold Macmillan, 'You've never had it so good!'. The Table D'hote has a broad range to choose from and at £24.50 for 4 courses is good value. Book 2 weeks in advance.

Open: Mon-Fri 12.00pm-2.00pm & 7.00pm-9.30pm last orders;
Sat 7.00pm-9.30pm;
Sun 12.00pm-2.00pm

Map ref: C2

New World Bistro

10/11, Front Street, **Shotley Bridge**
01207 508906

Price £28

Situated on the curve of Shotley Bridge's main street, the cream and burnt orange walls, the honey-coloured wood floors and muslin drapes present a fresh, modern feel. As the name implies, this bistro offers a cosmopolitan menu with everything from traditonal English dishes to exotic game and seafood recipes from around the world. Smoked breast of pigeon on coconut mashed potato or Aubergine, salami and mozzarella bake start things off. Main courses continue the pan global theme with Grilled loin of English lamb with a Mediterranean cassoulet bean sauce and Char-grilled shark steak with pasta verdi, sweet chilli and ginger sauce. Desserts like Apricot and whiskey bread and butter pudding and Passion fruit sorbet complete the journey. There are vegetarian and set menus for those who want a particular type of world tour. Bon voyage!

Open: Wed-Sat 7.00pm onwards;
Sat-Sun 12.00pm-1.30pm

Map ref: B1

Numjai

19, Millburngate Centre, **Durham City**
0191 386 2020

Price £2◂

The delicacy of Thai cuisine is brought to life in this excellent restaurant. Masterchef Pong Donchai displays his expertise with the quiet confidence that is his hallmark. The subtlety of the Tom Yam Pla, a sour and spicy soup, has to be tasted to be believed, as does the Koong Kra Bueng, crispy minced prawn pancakes wrapped with a spring roll pastry. This is oriental cooking of the highest order. Main course recipes bring chicken, meat and fish into a new and different light by blending the fierce bite of chilli with the gentle sweetness of coconut milk. This is also highly decorative cuisine and each dish is presented with sculpted fruit and vegetables: tomatoes and carrots as chrysanthemums and lotus blossoms. Delightful. Set on the river's edge in the heart of the city this has to be a must for anyone visiting Durham or lucky enough to live there. The set lunch menus (3 courses + coffee: £5.95) are superb value.

Map ref: C1   *Open: 7 days 11.30am-3.00pm &*
6.00pm-11.00pm

The Old Mill

Knitsley
01207 581642

Price £1◂

Looking out on a burbling mill race with the wooden mill wheel rhythmically rolling round, this restaurant has a character all its own. In summer diners can eat on the terrace beside the water and on cooler days there is a choice between the cosy stone-walled dining room or the light and airy conservatory. The menu carries a variety of cooking styles, from starters like Thai chilli dip and Garlic roasted potatoes to Stir fry duck in plum sauce and Mushroom stroganoff with rice. There is a selection of hefty steaks for the robust appetite. The trout comes straight from the Mill's own trout farm; it doesn't get much fresher than that! Desserts, Sticky Toffee and so on, are traditional sweet treats.

Map ref: B1   *Open: 7 days 11.30am-9.00pm*
last order

The Old Yard Tapas Bar

98, Bondgate, **Darlington**
01325 467385

Price £22 (5 tapas dishes)

The Old Yard has the authentic feel of a rustic Spanish bar, but in the centre of Darlington, which makes the contrast all the more acute. Low ceilings, muted Iberian music, torch wall-lights and rough-hewn tables make for a cosy, intimate atmosphere. The staff are very friendly and easy going and so is the food. Tasters of everything you can imagine can be combined to make your choice of meal. Chorizo, prawns, chicken wings, tuna croquettes and garlic bread all pile onto your plate. Take your pick from the 20+ dishes available plus the choice of blackboard specials. If, however, you want something different again, there is also a Greek meze menu with traditional Tzatziki, hummus, feta and olives. Baskets of bread, of course, come with everything. It's a good place to have an informal lunch out or to meet up with friends and enjoy the party atmosphere in the evenings.

Open: Sun-Fri 11.30am-2.30pm & 7.00pm-10.00pm; Sat 11.30am-10.30pm.

Map ref: C3

Oldfield's Restaurant

7, The Bank, **Barnard Castle**
01833 630700

Price £23.50

Oldfield's has a well established reputation for serving some of the best food for miles around. This award-winning restaurant was recognised early in it's career as a cut above the rest and continues to maintain a high standard of cuisine and service. The menus include classic and contemporary dishes combining local ingredients cooked with flair. Toulouse sausage stack on chestnut mash with a red onion marmalade or the interestingly named, Cullen Stink - a traditional Scottish smoked haddock soup, to start maybe. Main courses such as Soufflé of roquefort and hazelnuts on wilted leaves with drizzled walnut oil vinaigrette for vegetarians or a juicy Pork rump steak wrapped in dried ham on a bed of roast artichoke hearts for the carnivores. Desserts to lead you off the straight and narrow; a three-in-one with Warm sugared beignet with hot butterscotch sauce and vanilla ice cream or a simple Individual tart of sharp lemon custard with a crisp sugar glaze. No calories there then!

Open: Mon-Fri 11.30am-2.30pm & 6.00pm-9.30pm; Sat 11.00am-9.30pm; Sun 12.00-3.30pm

Map ref:B3

Durham

The Pavilion Cantonese Restaurant

Iveston, Consett
01207 503388

Price £29

The Pavilion is a very popular restaurant. The reason why is obvious; it's the quality. From the warm welcome and the relaxing sofas in the bar, to the attractive decor with etched glass panels screening the tables, everything demonstrates the attention to detail which is the hallmark of this restaurant. A wide range of dishes are carefully grouped into set meals for those who welcome a little guidance, with menus rising from The Pavilion Delight Banquet at £20.90 to the Imperial Banquet at £30.95. The King prawns with ginger and spring onions is a masterful blend of succulent seafood with mild spiced sauce. The Chicken with lemon sauce has all the crunch of a deep-fried dish with a fragrant lemon tang to balance the sauce's sweetness. Everything is served with great friendliness, which is why so many people keep on going back for more.

Map ref: B1   Open: 7 days 12.00pm-2.00pm & 6.00pm-11.00pm

The Raven Country Hotel

Ebchester
01207 562562

Price £24

Standing high on a hill, the long, glass-fronted dining room overlooks the valley where, at night, a trail of lights glitter along the road and glimmer in the villages away off in the distance. In summer it looks out over the canopy of trees and in winter there is an uninterrupted vista. A good view whichever time you come. The menu has a range of innovative dishes coming from a chef with a flair for the unusual. The Liver parfait with dressed leaves, onion jam and melba toast is a delicate mousse starter with character. I recommend the Guinea fowl brushed with orange and soy sauce, served with a terrine of rice with coconut milk for a main course. A delicious blend of flavours, but then so is the Grilled medallions of fillet steak with a red wine and shallot sauce, glazed with a rosemary and onion crust. And the desserts. See for yourself.

Map ref: B1   Open: Mon - Sat 12.00-2.00pm & 6.30-9.30pm: Sun 12.30-2.00pm

Redworth Hall

Redworth
01388 770600

Price £31

Redworth Hall is an imposing manor house, dating from the 17th century, situated in 25 acres of woodland. The hotel boasts two restaurants, The Blue Room for "fine dining" and the Conservatory, a modern brasserie with a contemporary menu. Up to the minute dishes such as Warm confit of duck leg with a crispy chorizo salad and mango dressing jostle alongside Deep fried brie wedges with sweet chilli sauce. Among the 14 entrées are Thai style green chicken curry with lemon scented rice and Mushroom risotto with parmesan shavings. Desserts feature favourites such as Sticky toffee pudding with fudge sauce and Redworth's own Passion fruit creme brulée. Coffee and a stroll around the grounds for the perfect finish to a great meal.

Open: 7 days 7.00pm-9.45pm   Map ref: B2

Rose & Crown

Romaldkirk
01833 650213

Price £30

The Saxon village of Romaldkirk is the beautiful setting for this award-winning restaurant. Each year the accolades pour in along with the AA rosettes and stars, and not surprisingly when you consider what is on offer. Keynote dishes, some supplied with recipes, focus on local produce and result in such delights as Poached hen's eggs on pan haggerty with leaf spinach and hollandaise; Roast fillet of Teesdale fell lamb with a potato and wild mushroom broth, black pudding and crostini and paloise sauce; Sautéed breasts of woodpigeon with compote of beetroot, caramelised shallots, chestnuts and juniperberry sauce. The intelligence and imagination behind these dishes is reflected in desserts such as Hot apricot tart with amaretto ice cream and Iced honey and whisky cream. Treat yourself and stay overnight in the R&C hotel and enjoy the breakfast too.

Open: Mon-Sat 7.30pm-9.00pm;   Map ref: B3
Sun 12.00pm-1.30pm

Open: Mon-Sat 7.30pm-9.00pm; Sun 12.00pm-1.30pm   *Map ref: B3*

Seaham Hall Hotel & Oriental Spa

Lord Byron's Walk, **Seaham**
0191 516 1400

Price £40

Past the fantastic water sculpture, through the curved glass doors and into the galleried foyer of Seaham Hall and you already have a clear impression of luxury and designer chic. The restaurant continues the theme. The light and spacious room with its winter white walls, chestnut chenille and suede seats and cream table linen, looks out onto a splendid terrace and landscaped parkland. Monumental mirrors reflect the view. The menu is just as sophisticated. A salad of Roasted quail with nut oil dressing or Mushroom boullion, woodpigeon and mushroom ravioli can be followed by Gressingham duck with caramelised apple and cinnamon scented jus or Fillet of beef with a mushroom mustard crust and Madeira sauce. Richly sweet desserts follow. The service is friendly and unobtrusive. Whatever they do the Seaham Hall standard is always there.

Map ref: C1   Open: 7 days 12.00pm-2.00pm & 7.00pm-9.30pm

Whitworth Hall Country Park Hotel - Silver Buckles Brasserie

Nr **Spennymoor**
01388 811772

Price £26

Whitworth Hall is the ancestral home of the legendary Bobby Shafto - he of silver buckles fame. The light and airy Victorian conservatory dining room with its private terrace, has fine views over the landscaped parkland with grazing deer and ornamental water features. The French-based menu offers a wide range of dishes from rustic and simple to rich and fancy. At one end is the Paté en campagnard, pork paté with fresh shallots, herbs and topped with forestiere mushrooms and onion marmalade. Among the entrées is Fresh oven roasted aubergine drizzled with pesto and stuffed with a risotto of pine nuts, chopped eggs and feta cheese placed on a puddle of pimento coulis. The somewhat flowery language is more direct when it comes to the richest dishes, the desserts. A dark chocolate mousse flavoured with Cointreau and topped with fresh cream and almonds. Straight and to the point.

Map ref: C2   Open: Mon-Sat 12.00pm-2.00pm; 7 days 6.30pm-9.30pm.

BEAVERS TEA ROOM
4 Market Place, Barnard Castle
Tel: (0 1833) 637634
Open 9am-5pm Tuesday to Sunday
High above the River Tees, Barnard Castle offers a stunning spectacle with its castle remains, cobbled streets, riverside walks and the famous Bowes Museum. Close to the Museum you will find Beavers Tea Room serving breakfasts and light snacks in traditional English style.
Map ref: B3

*BOWES CAFE
Bowes Museum, Barnard Castle
Tel: (01833) 690606   www.bowesmuseum.org.uk
Open 11am-4.30pm daily
This cafe is located within the beautiful Bowes Museum built in the style of French chateaux by John and Josephine Bowes. The café is designed as a country tea room and serves a good selection of main courses and snacks including vegetarian options.
Map ref: B3

BRIDGE END CAFE
4 Commercial Street, Willington
Tel: (01388) 746546
Open 8am-3pm (open later in summer months)
This cafe is located a few miles from Durham and Crook, easily accessible to the Binchester Roman Fort and serves a good selection of home-made light meals and delicious desserts including apple tea cakes, scones and ginger ice creams.
Map ref: B2

CASTLE GATE CAFE
8 Market Place, Bishop Auckland
Tel: (01388) 608770
Open 9am-4.30pm Monday to Saturday
This is a 16th century tea room with lots of character and offers traditional home-cooked English food with daily specials including mince beef with Yorkshire pudding. It is located next to the entrance of the Bishop Auckland Castle and a few miles from a Roman Fort at Binchester.
Map ref: B2

COUNTRY STYLE TEA ROOM
20 Market Place, Middleton in Teesdale
Tel: (01833) 640924   www.countrystyle2000.co.uk
This tea shop and bakery serves light snacks and cream teas and is renowned for its rum truffle cake, treacle tarts and home-made country vegetable soup. Located a few miles from High Force Waterfall and 'Meet the Middletons' Heritage Activity Centre.
Map ref: A2

DURHAM DALES CENTRE
Castle Gardens, Stanhope, Weardale
Tel:(01388) 527650
Open 10am-5pm daily (seasonal times may vary at weekends)
Specialising in home-made food including soups, sandwiches and puddings. The Dales Centre also includes a Tourist Information Centre, craft shops, beautiful Gardens and an animal trail.
Map ref: A2

FARMHOUSE KITCHEN
61 Church Street, Shildon
Tel: (01388) 775309
Open 9am-4pm daily
Located near to a heritage railway museum and Darlington this tea room prides itself on its home-cooked food in a traditional setting.
Map ref: B2

THE FROSTERLEY CRAFT FAIR AND TEA ROOMS
Front Street, Frosterley, Bishop Auckland
Tel: (01388) 526488
Open 1.30pm-6.30pm (check for seasonal opening) This tea room has an antique and collectors corner as well as a pretty courtyard and lots of walks and scenery to enjoy.
Map ref:B2

MAINSGILL FARM SHOP & TEA ROOM
East Layton, North Yorks
Tel: (01325) 718385 www.mainsgillfarm.co.uk
Open 9am-5pm daily
This farm shop sells home-made preserves and fresh meats, cheeses, fruits and vegetables, all of which you'll find in the tea room. You will find them near to Richmond, Barnard Castle and Darlington attractions. Also located next to Ravensworth Garden Centre.
Map ref: B3

PIERCEBRIDGE FARM ORGANICS
Piercebridge Farm, Durham
Tel (01325) 374251
Open daily - please ring prior to visit
This fairly new organic tea room serves home-made food and is a must for cyclists. The farm is situated in Piercebridge, a pretty village which lies on the site of a 3rd century Roman fort and has a farm shop selling fresh organic vegetables, fruit and meats.
Map ref: C1

*THORPE FARM PEEL HOUSE
Greta Bridge, Barnard Castle
Tel: (01833) 627242
Open Monday to Saturday 9am-5.30pm and Sunday 10am-5.30pm
This striking Georgian police house on the edge of the Yorkshire Dales and Teesdale and has already gained a reputation as a gourmet country deli and coffee shop. The features of the tea room include the original kitchen range and vaulted ceilings. Extensive range of food is served including a range of baked breads, dairy produce, pates and cheeses.
Map ref: B3

*TEESDALE HOTEL TEA ROOM
Market Place, Middleton in Teesdale
Tel:(01833) 640264   www.teesdalehotel.com
Open 11am-5.30pm daily
This tea room used to be the stable of a coaching inn (now the Teesdale Hotel) and can be found in a pretty courtyard. It offers a wide range of light meals and cream teas and is fully licensed.
Map ref: A2

Northumbria Tourist Board member

Places to eat in Tees Valley

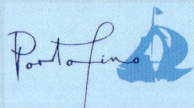

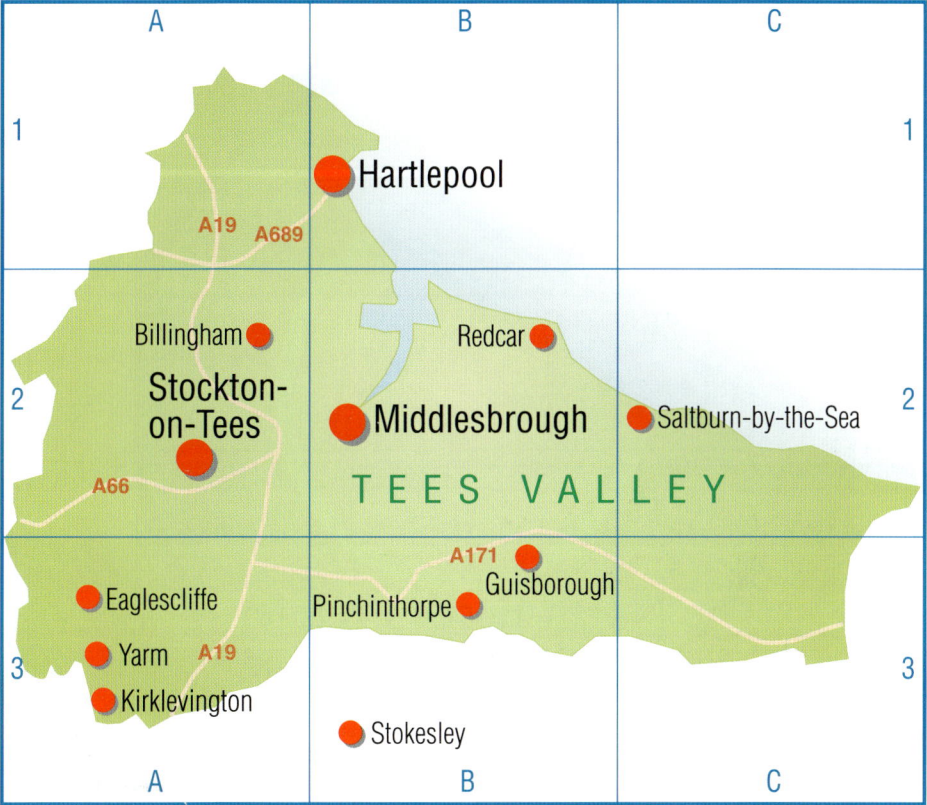

A   B   C

1   1

Hartlepool

A19   A689

Billingham   Redcar

Stockton-
on-Tees   Middlesbrough   Saltburn-by-the-Sea

2   2

A66   TEES VALLEY

A171
Guisborough
Eaglescliffe   Pinchinthorpe

3   Yarm   A19   3

Kirklevington

Stokesley

A   B   C

Al Syros

9, Upper Church Street, **Hartlepool**
01429 266233

Price £22

A pocket of Saharan warmth in the heart of the town, Al Syros is an oasis of exotic cuisine. The decor reflects the influences on the menu, with its dark blue ceiling for the desert sky, and yellow and rich ochre walls for the sandy earth. Offering a fusion of Algerian, Catalonian and Provencal dishes, the menu is varied and constantly changing. Starters include Chicken ballontine with hummus dressing and Fresh crab and mango salad. Tempting entrées like Seafood paella (claiming to be the best north of Barcelona!) and Tournedos of beef "belle forestiere" are followed by an array of desserts. Chef-owner, Didier, recommends the Fresh strawberry brochette with warm chocolate fondue. He samples all the wines himself and encourages you to do the same!

Open: Mon-Fri 12.00pm-1.30pm
& 5.30pm-9.30pm last orders:
Sat 7.00pm-9.30pm last orders

Map ref: B1

Chadwick's

104b, High Street, **Yarm**
01642 788558

Price £29

Tucked away on the end (or beginning) of Yarm village, Chadwick's has a reputation for outstanding food. The unprepossessing exterior and understated interior design of cream, burnt reds and marron, belie the treat in store. The menu speaks for itself. Where else will you find Serrano ham, manchego and figs as a starter or Black pudding spring rolls and pineapple chilli dunk? Refreshing combinations demonstrate the intelligence behind the dishes. Tournedos of salmon, spiced lentils, foie gras and apple chutney - I think I've made my point. The desserts force home the argument with delights such as Citrus cheesecake with blood orange sorbet and Chocolate, banana and toffee coupe. Set menus, (4 courses £37; 2 courses £27) both with coffee and petit fours, guide you through. You'll want coffee so you can sit back and revel in the memory.

Open: Mon-Sat 7.00pm - late   Map ref: A3

Gisborough Hall Hotel - Tocketts Restaurant

Whitby Lane, **Guisborough**
0870 400 8191

Price £32

A 19th century country house surrounded by landscaped gardens with manicured lawns and acres of woodland make a lovely setting for Tocketts. The menu adds substance to the appearance of the place with dishes such as Timbale of sole mousse filled with caviar with a shellfish bisque and Goats cheese en croute with a cherry tomato and pinenut salad. Entrées range from the traditional Medallions of beef on a horseradish mash with a red wine jus to a contemporary vegetarian Aubergine tower layered with Mediterranean vegetables. Desserts are equally eclectic with Lemon and raspberry brulée served with raspberry ripple ice cream contrasting well with the more filling Steamed syrup sponge with creme anglais. The set menus offer a good range of dishes and are good value.

Map ref: B3   Open: Mon-Sat 12.30pm-2.30pm;
Sun 12.30pm-3.30pm;
Sun-Thurs 7.00pm-9.30pm;
Fri-Sat 7.00pm-10.00pm.

Hide Café Bar Grill

Fairfax Court, 32-34, High Street, **Yarm**
01642 355558

Price £26

This ultra-modern café and bistro-style restaurant is tucked away in an equally contemporary shopping gallery on Yarm's main street. The upstairs dining room has a skylight, modern beechwood furniture and a decorative wall of wines at the bar area. The designer's hand is everywhere. The staff are young and lively and so is the menu. Beginning with dishes like Steamed mussels, chorizo sausage, peppers and tomato and Chicken liver and pistachio paste, toasted brioche and house chutney, the menu moves on to an impressive cast of main courses. Duck a l'orange sits comfortably next to Thai green vegetable curry with a good range of side dishes to choose from. Desserts are mainly old favourites. The buzzing atmosphere from the cafe downstairs adds to the ambience to make this worth a visit.

Map ref: A3   Open: 7 days 10.00am-10.00pm

Kirklevington Hall - Judges Restaurant

Kirklevington
01642 789000

Price £47

Kirklevington Hall is ideally placed for a break on the North York Moors. The ancient abbeys of Rievaulx and Rosedale are close by and there is plenty of good walking country at hand. To end the day in this very classy, award-winning restaurant would be perfect. Mozaic of duck, foie gras and pistachio nuts with toasted brioche followed by Turbot poached in wheat beer with langoustine tails might be your choice. Alternatively you may prefer Quail roasted with honey on bubble and squeak with morels and Loin of venison on a sauce poivrade with root vegetables. Desserts are equally rich with Hot chocolate fondant with a white chocolate sorbet vying with Brown sugar parfait with roasted figs and a port wine syrup. The sommelier has a wine list the size of a small book. Read and enjoy.

Open: 7 days 7.00pm-9.30pm; Sun-Fri 12.00pm-2.00pm

Map ref: A3

Krimo's

The Marina, **Hartlepool**
01429 266120

Price £22

Krimo's is more than just a restaurant. The bar is open to non-diners who want to while away an hour or two watching the yachts and fishing boats drift in and out of the marina. Diners have the same pleasure, alongside a meal to remember. The canopied, Moorish-style dining room looks out across the water and is the ideal setting for a relaxed lunch or dinner. The menu has a distinctly Algerian flavour with dishes like Boureks - spicy minced beef in crisp filo pastry with harissa mayonnaise as a starter and Fish tagine with vegetables and delicious chunks of fresh fish to follow. The cosmopolitan character of the menu is shown in the Fish soup with garlic croutons and entrées like Chicken breast stuffed with king prawns and a baby lobster sauce. Delicious desserts are there if you need more. Famous yachtspeople tie-up and settle down to a feast alongside the loyal regulars that Krimo, the owner, has collected over the years.

Open: Tues-Sat 12.00pm-1.30pm & 6.00pm-9.30pm last orders

Map ref: B1

Tim Beswick,
Real Meals, Saltburn-by-the-Sea

come and
DISCOVER OUR HOSPITALITY

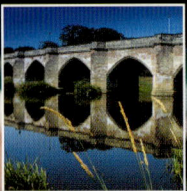

You're spoilt for choice when you visit Northumbria, not just by the tranquil countryside and historic cities, but by the wealth of restaurants on offer across the region.

As well as the hundreds of places to eat in Northumbria, why not take a trip out into the countryside and discover our quaint village tea rooms and farm shops?

Overflowing with traditional fayre, they serve delicious home-cooked food using recipes that have been passed down through the centuries and reveal the true flavour of Northumbria.

For more information call the Great North Number on **0191 375 3043.**
www.visitnorthumbria.com

NORTHUMBRIA
TOURIST BOARD

Lotus Garden

Unit 1, Navigation Point, **Hartlepool Marina**
01429 275527

Price £23

The modern setting of the marina is carried through in this highly contemporary, Oriental fusion restaurant. New meets old with two stone lions guarding the chrome-glass doors and gigantic, decorative vases standing sentry within. Comfy sofas in the bar area encourage diners to relax with a pre-dinner drink. Drifts of silk in electric pinks and blues provide splashes of colour on the walls with imaginative lighting enhancing them to full effect. Thai-Chinese-Japanese-Indonesian dishes flourish, too many to list here but Butterfly king prawns with a choice of sauces, Skewered fillet steak satay and Peking ribs jostle for attention next to Cantonese roast duck and Szechuan chicken. The chef delights in regional specialities like Stir fried won ton and Chicken with tender snow peas. It's poetry and the whole experience is brought together with live music (Wed-Sat).

*Open: 7 days 12.00pm-2.00pm &
Fri-Sun 6.00pm-12.00;
Mon-Thurs 6.00pm-11.30pm.*

Map ref: B1

Parkmore Hotel - Reeds at Six Three Six Restaurant

636, Yarm Road, **Eaglescliffe**
01642 786815

Price £23

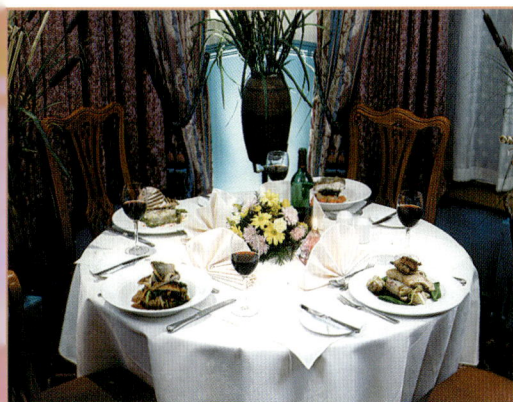

Behind the the Victorian facade of the hotel lies the 636 restaurant. The lunch and dinner menus blend traditional English cuisine with contemporary Mediterranean recipes to produce an interesting blend of dishes. Start with Peppered tuna steak with a garlic and lemon couscous and pickled cucumber or Hot smoked salmon, lemon and chive mousse with a lobster sauce and dressed herb salad. From the entrées you could choose Crispy seabass fillet with lemon crushed potatoes, broccoli, fried anchovies and a dill cream sauce or Chicken breast with black olive mash, wild mushrooms, asparagus and tomato veloute. The well spaced tables mean that you enjoy your own company even when this very popular restaurant is full, which, unsurprisingly, it usually is.

*Open: 7 days 12.00pm-2.00pm;
Mon-Sat 6.45pm-9.30pm;
Sun 6.30pm-9.00pm*

Map ref: A3

Pinchinthorpe Hall Hotel - Brewhouse Bistro

Pinchinthorpe
01287 630200

Price £27

This elegant, 17th century manor house holds plenty of surprises. The Hall's medieval moat surrounds the Georgian kitchen gardens and a 200 year old vine twists its way around the hothouse. The modern, organic micro brewery, which you can tour, is the source of the restaurant's and bistro's special beers. The bistro menu has a spread of cosmopolitan dishes ranging from the ubiquitous Thai fishcakes (lightly spiced and served with a Thai sauce) to Avocado vinaigrette with prawns to start. Moving on; entrées such as Fillet of salmon with herb butter sauce and a traditional Lamb shank with braised vegetables and bubble and squeak plus fresh fish dishes fit the bill. Desserts range from a Medley of fresh fruit with cream or live yoghurt to an interesting Cherry and coconut tart with Turkish delight ice cream. Something for everyone.

Map ref: B3   *Open: Mon-Sat 12.00pm-9.30pm;*
Sun 12.00pm-4.30pm.

Portofino

The Historic Quay, **Hartlepool Marina**
01429 266166

Price £22

The setting for this first floor restaurant could not be more dramatic, overlooking the Historic Quay and the old war ship, Trincomalee. The interior replicates an Italian piazza with highly decorative mosaics (courtesy of the creative owner, Krimo) who is also depicted as the chef of the 'piazza's' patisserie. Although Italian in feel, the menu is definitely eclectic, offering Algerian merguez sausages in a spicy tomato sauce with rice (the 'zing' is said to be highly addictive) and Cajun cod with tomato and chorizo sauce. Milder recipes like Breast of French duckling served pink with sweet blackcurrant and apple sauce are there for the less fiery amongst us. The menu also carries a full range of pizza-pasta and chicken dishes and a good value two course and Happy Hour meals.

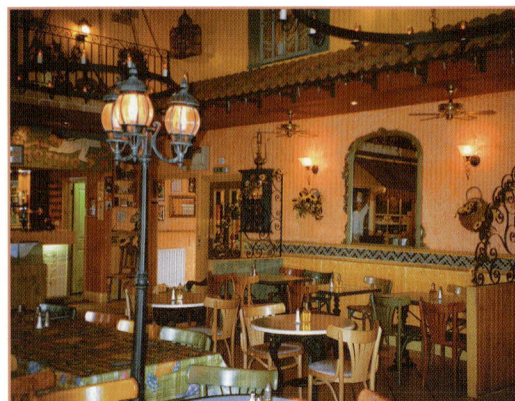

Map ref: B1   *Open: Tues-Sat 12.00pm-1.45pm*
& 5.30pm-10.00pm

Purple Onion Brasserie

80, Corporation Road, **Middlesbrough**
01642 222250

Price £30

A stone's throw from Middlesbrough's Riverside stadium, the Purple Onion Brasserie is a quirky mix of Parisien fin-de-siecle art and late Victorian bric-a-brac - but tasteful. The food is much more up to date and with a global character. Thai fish cakes sit alongside Roasted Italian vegetables and Swiss cheese croutons on the house soup. Entrées continue the theme with Grilled English duck breast with sun dried cherries, pistachios, couscous and crispy pancetta and Chargrilled sirloin steak accompanied with a range of sauces from au poivre to bernaise. Regular live music in the basement adds depth to your experience of the salsa. A cultured cosmopolitan experience.

Open: Mon- Sat 12.00pm-2.00pm & 5.00pm-10.0pm. Sun lunch only

Map ref: B2

The Waiting Room

9, Station Road, **Eaglescliffe**
01642 780465

Price £18

The super-relaxed, kitchen-friendly feel to this vegetarian restaurant just has to be experienced to be believed. The warmth of the staff, the wholesome food and a marvellous range of organic and fruit-based wines, beers and ciders (plus conventional ones too) demonstrate the owners' commitment to the freshest and the best - always. All the ingredients come fresh into and then out of the kitchen to make the Carrot and ginger soup, the Tomato, mozzarella and basil tart and the Guacamole with tortilla chips. Main courses like Hungarian mushroom goulash and Broccoli, leek and stilton pie (very popular with the men, apparently) are all cooked and served with care and imagination. The desserts are equally tempting with Chocolate and pineapple pudding and Baked custard tart making the running. If you pass this one by you are missing a treat and only have yourself to blame.

Open: Mon-Sat 11.00am-2.30pm & 7.00pm-9.30pm last orders

Map ref: A3

ANGEL TEA ROOMS
22 High Street, Stokesley
Tel: (01642) 713622
Open 9am-5.30pm
Serving home-cooked food with daily specials, the Angel is located on the High Street in Stokesley, close to the market (open Friday) and ideal after a walk on the Cleveland Hills. The neighbouring village is Great Ayton, the birthplace of Captain Cook.
Map ref: B3

MRS BRIDGE'S COFFEE SHOP
2 Cragton House, Queen Street, Redcar
Tel: (01642) 489818
Open 9.30am-5pm daily
Near to the coast, this coffee shop serves fresh sandwiches, home-made cakes and delicious scones - take your pick from wholemeal, apple and cinnamon, cherry and almond or fruit and cheese.
Map ref: B2

EMILY'S
71 Westgate, Guisborough
Tel: (01287) 630100
Open 9am-5pm daily
Located within the heart of Guisborough, this coffee shop serves all home-made hot and cold food with a good vegetarian selection. It's ideally situated during a visit to the Guisborough market on Tuesdays, Thursdays and Saturdays.
Map ref: B3

GOODBODY'S
58 Albert Road, Middlesbrough
Tel: (01642) 640299
Open 8.15am-3.30 daily (closed Saturday)
This coffee shop and restaurant serves a healthy and imaginative menu of light snacks and main meals with extremely popular veggie burgers. Their slogan 'Exercise a little wisdom - Eat at Goodbodys' demonstrates this. You'll find them near to the Town Hall in Middlesbrough.
Map ref: B2

MCCOYS
44 High Street, Yarm
Tel: (01642) 791234
Open 9am-5pm
Nestling within the loop of the River Tees, Yarm is a place not to be missed. With its elegant Georgian architecture and olde worlde charm, it's easy to see why it's a favourite with film producers. It has an extensive range of restaurants and coffee shops, one of which is McCoys serving lunches, delicious hot and cold food, and is near to many local gift shops.
Map ref: A3

PRIORY COFFEE HOUSE
2 Chaloner Mews, Guisborough
Tel: (01287) 635284
Open 9am-5.30pm daily (closed Sunday)
Located in the medieval market town of Guisborough, the Priory is a five minute walk from the ruins of an ancient priory. It's also on the Captain Cook Trail, which starts at Great Ayton and goes through to Whitby. They serve all home-baked food including steak pies, lasagnes and vegetarian. Outside eating is also available in the summer.
Map ref: B3

SIGNALS COFFEE SHOP
Station Square, Saltburn
Tel: (01287) 622982
Open 8pm-5pm daily
A fashionable spa in 1861, Saltburn remains largely unchanged and still retains its Victorian splendour with elegant houses set high above the sea. Located in the centre of Saltburn this coffee shop is ideal after a stroll on the beach or a visit to Valley Gardens or the local Woodland Centre. They serve a good selection of home cooked food and don't forget to try their delicious Yorkshire cheesecake.
Map ref: C2

VIRGOS
7 Dundas Street, Saltburn
Tel: (01287) 624031
Open 9am-5pm Monday to Saturday.
This modern tea room is located in the centre of Saltburn, a few minutes from the beach and serves some delicious home-made light snacks, hot meals and coffees.
Map ref: C2

WINDLEBRIDGE TEA ROOM
Windlebridge Nursery, Middlesbrough Road, Guisborough **Tel (01287) 635642**
Open Monday to Saturday 10am-4pm Sunday from 11am-4pm.
This tea room is located within the nursery and offers excellent views onto The Roseberry Topping hills. It serves a high proportion of home-cooked food such as snacks and light lunches.
Map ref: B3

YUCKERS (used to be called Village Tea Rooms)
45 Station Road, Billingham
Tel: (01642) 361563
Open 7.30am -2.30pm
Located in the village of Billingham near to Stockton and Middlesbrough, Yuckers is very popular with ramblers as it's near to Billingham Beck Valley Walkway. They serve a good selection of home-made food including traditional meals such as mince pie and dumpling.
Map ref: A2

Farmers markets are becoming increasingly popular in Northumbria as an excellent way of promoting and selling locally produced food and crafts.

The main emphasis of the markets is to help local producers and processors to sell their goods direct to the public, near the source of origin, creating benefits to them and the local community.

Farmers markets are fun for all the family and make shopping a sociable and enjoyable experience, not to mention their help in improving diet and nutrition by providing access to fresh food. They also stimulate local economic development by increasing employment and encouraging consumers to support local business.

Here's where you'll find your nearest farmers market -

*ALNWICK - last Friday monthly
9am - 2pm Town Square
Contact Brian Crosby   **Tel: 01670 825895** or
07947 323396
Email: brian@crosby56.fsnet.co.uk

*BARNARD CASTLE - 1st Saturday monthly
10am - 3pm Market Square
Contact: Cathie Tinn   **Tel: 0771 967 3739**
Email: cathietinn@glenridge.freeserve.co.uk

*BISHOP AUCKLAND - 2nd Friday monthly
10am - 4pm Market Place
Contact: Cathie Tinn   **Tel: 0771967 3739**
Email: cathietinn@glenridge.freeserve.co.uk

BLYTH- 2nd Tuesday monthly
Market Place
Contact: George Tucker   **Tel: 01670 542306**
Email: gtucker@blythvalley.gov.uk

CHESTER-LE-STREET- 1st Tuesday monthly
9am - 2.30pm, Market Place
Contact: Jim Holmes **Tel:0191 3871805**

*DARLINGTON - 3rd Friday monthly
9am - 4pm Market Square, Town Centre
Contact: Peter Wilson   **Tel: 01325 388691**
Email: peter.wilson@darlington.gov.uk

DURHAM - 3rd Thursday monthly
10am - 4pm   Market Place
Contact: Eileen Wood **Tel: 0191 3846153**
E-mail: eileen@durhammarkets.co.uk

*HEXHAM- 2nd Saturday monthly
9.30am - 1.30pm Market Square (Summer)
Auction Mart (Winter)
Contact: Julie Charlton   **Tel: 01434 270393** or
0789 0027613
Email: hallshill@tinyonline.co.uk

*MORPETH - 1st Sunday monthly
10.30am 'till sold out (c 1.30pm) Town Hall
Contact: Jim Pendrich   **Tel: 01670 514351**
Email: jpendrich@castlemorpeth.gov.uk

*PONTELAND- 4th Saturday monthly
9.30am till sold out (c 1pm) County High School
Contact: Jim Pendrich   **Tel: 01670 514351**
Email: jpendrich@castlemorpeth.gov.uk

*NEWCASTLE- 1st Friday monthly
9.30 - 2.30pm, Earl Grey Monument
Contact: Heather Thurlaway **Tel: 0191 2115533**
Email: property@newcastle.gov.uk

*SOUTH SHIELDS- every Wednesday, Easter to
Christmas, 9am - 4pm, Market Place
Contact: Andy Whittaker **Tel: 0191 4272063**
Email: andrew.whittaker@s-tyneside-mbc.gov.uk

TYNEMOUTH - 3rd Saturday monthly
9am - 4pm Tynemouth Metro Station
Contact: Christina Watson   **Tel: 0191 265 9971**

* Members of the National Association of Farmers Markets.

National Association of
FARMERS MARKETS

The National Association of Markets, South Vaults, Green Park Station, Green Park Road, Bath, BA1 1JB   www.farmersmarkets.net

*The*Journal

At the heart of the region

Northumberland

The Apple Inn
Lucker, Belford
Tel: 01668 213450
www.alnwickcastle.com/holidaycottages
Welcoming, cosy country pub with small restaurant offering home cooked food .

The Bark Pots
9 West End, Craster
Tel: 01665 576286 www.barkpots.co.uk
See recommended Tea Rooms in the Northumberland section.

The Bengal Cottage
Dene Moor, Shilbottle, Alnwick
Tel: 01665 575880
Indian restaurant serving authentic cuisine.

Brockbushes Farm Shop and Tea Room
Corbridge
Tel: 01434 633100 www.brockbrushes.co.uk
See recommended Tea Rooms in the Northumberland section.

The Byre Tea Room
Harbottle nr Rothbury
Tel: 01669 650476 www.the-byre.co.uk
See recommended Tea Rooms in the Northumberland section.

Canty's Brig
Near Paxton, Berwick-upon-Tweed
Tel: 01289 386255
Riverside pub, one mile from A1 at Berwick. Floodlit gardens and open fire. Serves homemade, fresh local food in a bistro style.

Charlies Fish & Chips
Albert Street, Amble by the sea
Tel: 01665 710206 www.charlieschips.co.uk
www.charlieschips.com
Take-away and licensed Restaurant. Holder of Seafish Friers Quality Award and Investors in People.

Doxford Country Store
Doxford Farm, Chathill
Tel: 01665 579477 www.doxfordfarmcottages.com
See recommended Tea Rooms in the Northumberland section.

Leaplish Lakeside Lodge
Kielder Water
Tel: 01434 250312
Restaurant and bar with stunning panoramic views over Kielder Water.

Marina Arms
The Wynd, Amble by the Sea
Tel: 01665 710094 www.marina-arms.ntb.org.uk
Family pub and 70 seater restaurant and games room. Adventure playground.

Milfield Country Cafe and Country Store
Main Road, Milfield, Wooler
Tel: 01668 216323
See recommended Tea Rooms in the Northumberland section.

Northumberland Cheese Farm & Coffee Shop
Make Me Rich Farm, Blagdon, Seaton Burn
Tel: 01670 789798
See recommended Tea Rooms in the Northumberland section.

Oxford Farm Shop and Tea Rooms
Ancroft, Berwick-upon-Tweed
Tel: 01289 387253
See recommended Tea Rooms in the Northumberland section.

Pebbles
Shield Street, Allendale
Tel: 01434 683975
See recommended Tea Rooms in the Northumberland section.

Ramblers Country House Restaurant
Farnley, Corbridge
Tel: 01434 632424
Restaurant within attractive country house, one mile from historic Corbridge.

The Ridley Arms
Stannington
Tel: 01670 789 216 www.SJF.co.uk
Once an 18th century coach house, this country pub maintains a warm, traditional yet contemporary feel with beautiful beer garden.

The Rob Roy Pub/Restaurant
Dock Road, Tweedmouth, Berwick-upon-Tweed
Tel: 01289 306428 www.therobroy.co.uk
Cosy pub, winner of food awards and specialising in seafood and Border produced meats.

Roseden Farm Shop
Wooperton, Alnwick
Tel: 01668 217271
See recommended Tea Rooms in the Northumberland section.

The Three Wheat Heads
Main Street, Thropton, Morpeth
Tel: 01669 620262
Country Inn with a la carte restaurant.

Travellers' Rest
Slaley
Tel: 01434 673231
www.travellersrest.sagesite.co.uk
Pub and restaurant serving freshly prepared food
and offering stunning views of the countryside,
rustic playground and beautiful garden.

The Valley Indian Restaurant
Old Station House, Station Road, Corbridge
Tel: 01434 633434 www.northeastonline.co.uk/valley
See recommended restaurants in the Northum-
berland section.

Well House Coffee Shop
33 High Street, Belford
Tel: 01668 213779
www.wellhousebelford.co.uk
Traditional coffee shop serving light meals and
refreshments.

County Durham

Austin's Bar and Bistro
Durham County Cricket Club, Chester le Street
Tel: 0191388 3335
Bar and bistro located in an attractive setting
within the grounds of the cricket club.

Bimbi's Restaurant
29-33 Neville Street, Durham
Tel: 0191 384 6470
This is a fish and chip restaurant that's open daily.

The Bridge Inn
1 Gordon Lane, Ramshaw, Evenwood, West
Auckland, Bishop Auckland
Tel: 01388 832509
Bar and restaurant with marvellous countryside
views and childrens' play area. Restaurant
serves a la carte and bar snacks.

Durham Dales Centre
Castle Gardens, Stanhope
Tel: 0191 01388 527650
See review in recommended Tea Rooms in the
Durham section.

The Countryman Inn
Bolam, Darlington
Tel: 01388 834577

Picturesque pub offering lunch and dinner with
fine ales. They have a paddock for caravan stor-
age and a beer garden.

The Coach House Café at Eggleston Hall
Eggleston, Barnard Castle
Tel: 01833 650432
Cafe serving delicious home-made calorific
treats, light lunches and snacks located next to a
gift shop.

Eastern Bamboo Chinese Restaurant
194 Northgate, Darlington
Tel: 01325 461607
Oriental restaurant serving Chinese food with
friendly service.

Emilio's Restaurant
96 Elvet Bridge, Durham
Tel: 0191 384 0096
Located within the historic Chapel of St Andrew
dating back to the 11th century.

Hamsterley Forest Tea Rooms
Hamsterley Forest, Bedburn, Bishop Auckland
Tel: 01388 488822
This quaint tea room serves freshly prepared light
snacks and cakes.

**The Four Seasons Restaurant/Shaftoe's
Restaurant/The Silver Buckle Bistro**
Whitworth Hall Country Park Hotel, Spennymoor
Tel: 01388 811772
www.whitworthhall.co.uk
Pub, brasserie and restaurant, located within
Whitworth Hall Country Park Hotel appealing to
all tastes, for business or pleasure.

Malt Shovel Inn & Lazy Shamrock Restaurant
Low Wham, Butterknowle, Bishop Auckland
Tel: 01388 710033
Bar/restaurant located close to Gaunless Valley
Visitor centre and Teesdale area.

Thorpe Farm Peel House
Greta Bridge, Barnard Castle
Tel: 01833 627242
See recommended Tea Rooms in the Durham
section.

Travellers' Rest Pub & Restaurant
Durham Road, Witton, Durham
Tel: 0191 371 0458
Small country village pub offering traditional ales
and bar meals.

Tees Valley

The King's Head Bistro
Market Place, Middleton-in-Teesdale
Tel: 01833 640467
www.kingsheadbistro.co.uk
Old pub turned bistro, close to attractions and
Tourist Information Centre.

Tyne & Wear

Blackfriars Café Bar
Low Friar Street (off Stowell Street), Newcastle
Tel: 0191 261 5945
www.blackfriarscafebar.co.uk
See recommended Restaurants in the Tyne &
Wear section.

Café Royal
8 Nelson Street, Newcastle
Tel: 0191 231 3000
Cafe and restaurant with deli selling a wide range
of produce.

Fisherman's Lodge Restaurant
Jesmond Dene, Newcastle
Tel: 0191 281 3281
See recommended Restaurants in the Tyne &
Wear section.

Matcham's Restaurant
Theatre Royal, Grey Street
Tel: 0191 2442513
www.theatre-royal-newcastle.co.uk
Beautiful refurbished restaurant within the theatre serving modern British cuisine. Also available is Café 100 for coffees and light bites.

Rupali Restaurant
6 Bigg Market, Newcastle
Tel: 0191 2328629
Very popular Indian restaurant in the heart of the
party district.

Twin Farms Pub
Kingston Park, Newcastle upon Tyne
Tel: 0191 2864500
Pub and restaurant renovated from two farm
buildings serving traditional food either in library,
bar or lounge with open log fires.

Shiremoor House Farm
Shiremoor, North Shields
Tel: 0191 257 6302
www.sjf.co.uk
See recommended Restaurants in the Tyne &
Wear section.

Sidney's Restaurant
Percy Park Road, Tynemouth
Tel: 0191 257 8500 www.sidneys.co.uk
See recommended Restaurants in the Tyne &
Wear section.

Cumbria

Gossipgate Gallery Coffee Shop
The Butts, Alston
Tel: 01434 381806 www.gossipgate.com
Small, intimate coffee shop serving wholefood
cakes and biscuits, located within Gossipgate
Gallery which specialises in local arts and crafts.

Keys to symbols:

- Vegetarian menu
- Children welcome
- Groups catered for
- Credit cards accepted
- No smoking area
- Accessible/or partially
  accessible for wheelchair users

The Northumbria Tourist Board has not vetted these
restaurants. Any complaints would have to be taken up
with the establishment direct. The Board will not enter
into dialogue or correspondence regarding complaints.
Every effort has been made to ensure that the information is correct, but Northumbria Tourist Board cannot
accept responsibility in respect of any error or omission,
which may have occurred.

Whether you are on holiday or on business in the region, Northumbria's Tourist Information Centres (TIC's) offer friendly, local advice and information. If you require further information on the area, please contact or call in to one of the Tourist Information Centres listed below

TYNE & WEAR

GATESHEAD
Central Library, Prince Consort Road
Tel: (0191) 477 3478

GATESHEAD METROCENTRE
Portcullis & The Arcade
Tel: (0191) 460 6345

GATESHEAD QUAYS
St Mary's Church, Oakwellgate, Gateshead
Tel: (0191) 460 6345

NEWCASTLE AIRPORT
Main Concourse
Tel: (0191) 214 4422

NEWCASTLE UPON TYNE
132 Grainger Street
Tel: (0191) 277 8000
Central Station
Tel: (0191) 277 8000

NORTH SHIELDS
Unit 18, Royal Quays Outlet, Shopping Centre
Tel: (0191) 200 5895

SOUTH SHIELDS
Museum & Gallery, Ocean Road
Tel: (0191) 454 6612

SOUTH SHIELDS
Amphitheatre, Sea Road
Tel: (0191) 455 7411

SUNDERLAND
50 Fawcett Street
Tel: (0191) 553 2000

WHITLEY BAY
Park Road
Tel: (0191) 200 8535

NORTHUMBERLAND

ADDERSTONE
Adderstone Services, A1 near Belford
Tel: (01668) 213678

ALNWICK
2 The Shambles
Tel: (01665) 510665

AMBLE
Queen Street Car Park
Tel: (01665) 712313

BELLINGHAM
Fountain Cottage, Main Street
Tel: (01434) 220616

BERWICK-UPON-TWEED
106 Marygate
Tel: (01289) 330733

CORBRIDGE
Hill Street
Tel: (01434) 632815

CRASTER
Craster Car Park
Tel: (01665) 576007

HALTWHISTLE
Railway Station, Station Road
Tel: (01434) 322002

HEXHAM
Wentworth Car Park
Tel: (01434) 652220

MORPETH
The Chantry, Bridge Street
Tel: (01670) 511323

ONCE BREWED
Northumberland National Park
Centre, Military Road, Bardon Mill
Tel: (01434) 344396

OTTERBURN
Otterburn Mill Visitor Centre
Tel: (01830) 520093

ROTHBURY
Northumberland National Park Centre,
Church Street
Tel: (01669) 620887

SEAHOUSES
Seafield Road Car Park
Tel: (01665) 720884

WOOLER
The Cheviot Centre, 12 Padgepool
Place
Tel: (01668) 282123

COUNTY DURHAM

BARNARD CASTLE
Woodleigh Flatts Road
Tel: (01833) 630272

BEAMISH
The North of England
Open Air Museum
Tel: (0191) 370 2533

BISHOP AUCKLAND
Town Hall, Market Place
Tel: (01388) 604922

DURHAM CITY
Gala Theatre, Millennium Place
Tel: (0191) 384 3720

MIDDLETON-IN-TEESDALE
10 Market Place
Tel: (01833) 641001

PETERLEE
20 The Upper Chare
Tel: (0191) 586 4450

STANHOPE
Durham Dales Centre, Castle Gardens
Tel: (01388) 527650

TEES VALLEY

DARLINGTON
13 Horsemarket
Tel: (01325) 388666

GUISBOROUGH
Priory Grounds, Church Street
Tel: (01287) 633801

HARTLEPOOL
Hartlepool Arts Centre, Church Square
Tel: (01429) 869706

MIDDLESBROUGH
99-101 Albert Road
Tel: (01642) 358086

REDCAR
West Terrace, Esplanade
Tel: (01642) 471921

SALTBURN
3 Station Buildings, Station Square
Tel: (01287) 622422

STOCKTON-ON-TEES
Theatre Yard, Off High Street
Tel: (01642) 393936

Tourist Information

Look out for this sign to be assured of a
warm and helpful welcome.

Key to symbols:

Seasonal opening, check with TIC for details

Some facilities for the disabled

Welcome Host - Staff at this TIC have attended
a training course on promoting high standards
of service and customer care.

Report form

To The Editor,

The Journal Guide to Eating Out, The Journal Newspaper, Groat Market, Newcastle upon Tyne NE1 1ED

I think the following restaurant/café should/should not be included in the next edition of The Journal Guide to Eating Out.

Name of establishment:

Address:

Postcode:

Reason:

I am not connected in any way with the management or proprietors of the above establishment

Name:

Address:

Signed

Date

Postcode:

Photocopies may be used.

Report Form

To The Editor,

The Journal Guide to Eating Out, The Journal Newspaper, Groat Market, Newcastle upon Tyne NE1 1ED

I think the following restaurant/café should/should not be included in the next edition of The Journal Guide to Eating Out .

Name of establishment:

Address:

Postcode:

Reason:

I am not connected in any way with the management or proprietors of the above establishment

Name:

Address:

Signed

Date

Postcode:

Photocopies may be used.

Report form

To The Editor,

The Journal Guide to Eating Out, The Journal Newspaper, Groat Market, Newcastle upon Tyne NE1 1ED

I think the following restaurant/café should/should not be included in the next edition of The Journal Guide to Eating Out.

Name of establishment: _____

Address: _____

_____

Postcode: _____

Reason: _____

_____

_____

_____

_____

_____

_____

_____

_____

_____

_____

_____

I am not connected in any way with the management or proprietors of the above establishment

Name: _____

Address: _____   Signed _____

_____   Date _____

Postcode: _____

Photocopies may be used.

Index

Index